THINKING ABOUT
Suicide?

A Book for the Suicidal Mind

to Achieve a new Life

Amora Grace

© Copyright 2022 - **All rights reserved.**

The content contained within this book may not be reproduced, duplicated or transmitted without direct written permission from the author or the publisher.

Under no circumstances will any blame or legal responsibility be held against the publisher, or author, for any damages, reparation, or monetary loss due to the information contained within this book, either directly or indirectly.

Legal Notice:

This book is copyright protected. It is only for personal use. You cannot amend, distribute, sell, use, quote or paraphrase any part, or the content within this book, without the consent of the author or publisher.

Disclaimer Notice:

Please note the information contained within this document is for educational and entertainment purposes only. All effort has been executed to present accurate, up to date, reliable, complete information. No warranties of any kind are declared or implied. Readers acknowledge that the author is not engaged in the rendering of legal, financial, medical or professional advice. The content within this book has been derived from various sources. Please consult a licensed professional before attempting any techniques outlined in this book.

By reading this document, the reader agrees that under no circumstances is the author responsible for any losses, direct or indirect, that are incurred as a result of the use of the information contained within this document, including, but not limited to, errors, omissions, or inaccuracies.

TABLE OF CONTENTS

Introduction 1

Chapter 1: Recognize the Problem and Understand Your Pain 5

    Defining the Problem 9

    You're not Alone 17

    Seek Solution but not Self-Harm 20

    Important Details to Remember 22

Chapter 2: Know How not to Give a F*ck 23

    You Are Imperfect but Still Valuable 26

    Know What Triggers You 32

    Protecting Your Headspace by Learning to Say "No" 34

    Know When and Where to Give a F*ck 38

    Important Details to Remember 39

Chapter 3: The Power of Forgiveness 41

    Why the Grudge? 42

    Trust the Process and Be Patient 48

    Heal Through Forgiveness 54

    Important Details to Remember 60

Chapter 4: Gratitude Inventory 62

    Obstacles in the Way of Leading a Grateful Life 65

    Tools and Exercises 69

        Keep a Gratitude Journal 69

        Writing Gratitude Letters 70

        Meditate/Pray With Gratitude 71

        Stop-Look-Go 72

Gratefulness Comes Before Happiness 75
Important Details to Remember 78

Chapter 5: Your Beliefs—Finding the Missing Power 80

Who/What Is the Higher Power? 83
How to Believe? 85
    Why Have Faith? 87
Important Details to Remember 96

Chapter 6: The Mantras You Need 98

Affirmations 99
    When You Are Feeling Depressed 101
    When You Are Feeling Anxious/Angry/Sad/Frustrated 102
    When You Are Feeling Hopeless and/or Worthless 102
    When You Are not Feeling Good in Your Body 103
    When You Feel Tired of Life 104
    When You Are Being Patronized 104
Meditative Chanting 105
Christian Meditation 109
Important Details to Remember 116

Chapter 7: Self-Love 117

How to Love Yourself 119
How to Heal With Self-Love 125
Important Details to Remember 128

Chapter 8: Meaningful Goals and the Power of Giving 130

How to Approach Your Goals 133
Which Goals Can Be Meaningful for You? 137
Share Your Love and Kindness 140
Important Details to Remember 146

Chapter 9: Real-Life Stories to Inspire You..................................148

    Carter Gaskins' Struggle...149

    Kjersta's Story of Hope..151

    Dess Butler's Experience With the Spirit of Suicide.......................154

    Celebrities Who Survived Suicide 157

        Owen Wilson...157

        Drew Barrymore 158

    Key Takeaways 159

Conclusion..160

References 165

This book is dedicated to you–the person who feels empty and lost, who needs understanding and love. Congratulations on taking a step toward your happiest self. Yes, you can get through this. You are in the right place, and I can't wait for you to see your wonderful life ahead.

INTRODUCTION

Suicide isn't losing a battle to live. It's losing the epic fight against a mind that begs you to die. —Anonymous

If you have picked up this book for yourself, this choice of yours is the same as you giving life a chance. You have already taken the first step, and with my help, you will be fully equipped with the skills and knowledge needed to live a hopeful life. After reading this book, you will learn to take care of the core issues within yourself, notice red flags, and look toward your bright future. I know that it takes a lot of courage to keep going on, and it can be even more difficult to bring about a change. I also know that you are courageous, you are fearless, and willing to face your future. Just keep reading and try to commit to reading this book for at least ten minutes a day. If you keep your heart and mind open to this book, it will transform you into a happier and more satisfied person who is devoted to life.

I know the feeling of hopelessness quite well. The feeling that your family and friends will be better off without you; that you're a burden on this world; that you cannot win against depression. This is exactly how depression works and when it gets the best of you, it feels like the only option is to end your life. My life, too, has been a constant battle and I would not wish it on anyone. This pain was my motivation for writing this book. I wanted to help you gain power over your depression and help you regain your life. You already have this power within you, you just need to bring it to life, and I promise, I'll be with you at every step.

At one point in my life, I was fascinated by death as well. It looked very appealing when compared with all that life had to offer me. I would often hope that someone would kill me or wish I would get shot in some mass shooting. Our thoughts can find the darkest corners of our minds, but we can bring them to light as well. Now, when I look back, I feel so blessed to have come out of that darkness. Today, I feel alive and am a completely different person, and I would love for you to experience the same. Suicide is increasing and it breaks my heart every time someone loses their life to it. But you will not be this person. It is time to make a change.

Now that I am a different person altogether, I have kept a diary containing all my Mantras and affirmations with me, so that I can defeat my negative thoughts and bring out the inherent strength that I have. Because of these mantras, I can be assured that I am capable of facing any difficulty that may come ahead. In all likelihood, when you reach the end of the book, you would be able to do this too.

I have carefully put together these chapters for you so that our end goal can be broken into smaller and more achievable goals. These effective steps and concepts have already helped thousands of people recover from alcoholism through the 12 steps by Alcoholics Anonymous. These steps can help you too. Every chapter in this book will help you get rid of your undesirable habits and behaviors, and instill the good values and qualities that you were born with. These steps require conscious effort and commitment on your end, a commitment to a promising future. I am positive that you will see results and see a change within yourself in as little as 30 days.

All nine chapters in this book are equally important for you to bring about this change. This is your sign to put in some effort, no matter what your life has been up until now. Your background does not matter here; you can be of any ethnicity, a man, a woman, a teenager, single, or divorced. What matters is your commitment to changing your status quo and what you do about it. Are you happy with the way your life is right now? Do you want to create a new life and a fresh perspective to improve your self-worth? This is probably the most valuable time of your life as you are standing on a cusp, and one step in any direction could completely transform you. I want you to take a step towards the best life that you are yet to live.

There is a Buddhist saying that the more logs you put into the fire, the higher the flames will be, which means, you must use your pain as fuel to energize your life and create higher flames of happiness. There is no better time to start something this transformational and positive than now. I promise you will have the life that you wanted, you will have peace and happiness but only when you start working on yourself. This book will help you get rid of your undesirable habits and behaviors and instill the good values and qualities that you were born with. Take this steps one day at a time. These steps require your conscious effort and commitment, the commitment to a promising future. So, let's begin our journey and start climbing up toward the light.

CHAPTER 1: RECOGNIZE THE PROBLEM AND UNDERSTAND YOUR PAIN

It starts working for you, when you decide it's true for you.

I heard this from a pastor named John G. Lake and could resonate with it instantly. Especially, when it comes to pain it becomes imperative that we know what our truth is. We are living and thinking human beings, and it is perfectly normal for us to feel regret/guilt/anger/sadness. But keeping your pain inside, letting it ferment instead of recognizing and dealing with it, can prove to be your downfall. This is why it's important to recognize your problem and understand your pain.

When it comes to the problem that led us to be this depressive, we just have to know two things about depression: One, it is caused by chemical imbalances which can be genetic, and second, it can be caused by our unmet psychological needs (like, sense of purpose, sense of belongingness, feeling loved, and valued). When we know about these two causes of depression, it becomes a little easier for us to identify where our own problems have risen from.

When it comes to pain, it can be tricky sometimes, and difficult to manage. If you do not control pain, it will start controlling you. It will control your thoughts and your behavior, making you think about ending it all, or making you think that you are not good enough. But we must push forward and recognize that pain is not our master, it is just a leech. Our subconscious should be our master. You must have heard your subconscious when it tells you to fight the pain. You must have faced these two opposing trains of thought, one positive and one negative. It feels like you have both the Angel and the devil inside you. Please know that your Angel is stronger than the Devil. Your subconscious is part of your body and you can easily control your subconscious.

There are two sides to the coin of pain—one is the victim and the other one is the victor. It is your choice which side you want to see and which side you want facing the other way. Which side do you think will help you fight your pain? Embrace the victor side, turn your greatest pain into your greatest achievement by acknowledging it, and then fighting it. You are not a victim, so, you are not to be pitied. You are an abundance of strength, courage, and love and these three qualities make you the victor. Maybe your greatest pain is not even about you, maybe it's about a greater purpose that you can only fulfill when you get over this cycle of pitying yourself. In my experience, I have understood that getting over my pain empowered me to help others who were suffering like me, and to bring light into others' lives. It is only because of winning over my pain that I could fully realize my purpose on this Earth.

So how do you gain an upper hand over your pain? The first step is to train your mind to recognize your emotions as they build up in you. For instance, you were belittled at a public event, and it is giving way for anger to rise in you. Imagine your anger coming up from your gut towards your brain. Your emotions will always try to go up to your brain to gain control. But if you train your brain to recognize the emotion coming up, it will show the emotion the light of consciousness, which will make it impossible for it to rise up and reach your brain. And when it does not reach your brain, it cannot control you. That pain/fear/anger would not be able to control your behavior, or your actions anymore. Therefore, this recognition is vital for you to control your pain.

We are talking about controlling the pain, not about killing it. You must have heard the saying "No pain, no gain," it is absolutely correct. Healing does not begin when the pain is over. Experiencing and feeling the pain is part of the healing process. It is an inescapable component of your path to success. It is just like working out your muscles, until and unless you don't feel the pain in your muscle while training, you would not see any results. You need to pinpoint where the exercise needs to hurt you and then redirect your exercise, so that you feel the pain as it is the only way to grow your muscle and make your body stronger. Then why can't we apply the same logic to our mental suffering?

So, when you honor the pain and feel it, your healing process will begin immediately. But there are rules when trying to recognize your pain, which Hal Elrod talks about in his 5-minute rule. We will talk about this method in detail in the next section. What you need to acknowledge right now is that maybe you've not been facing the truth which has led to you denying the possible solutions, leading to the worsening of the situation. I suggest you cram your head with the phrase—confrontation will empower me" and you will start seeing a difference soon. Close this book for a second and repeat this to yourself—"Confrontation will empower me. I can do this."

Now that we have understood why we should recognize our problems and understand our pain, I believe we must move on to the methodology we can use to achieve it.

Defining the Problem

Our brains are constantly thinking about something. The thoughts run through our minds like streaming services when the Wi-Fi is fast. Sometimes, we don't even know when we are thinking and how much we are thinking. In some cases, we have so much pain and negativity, that we can often find our thoughts to have a negative tone as well. But we can shift the negative stories going on in our minds to positive ones. Here, a connection with yourself is of utmost importance. There is a quote by Sathya Sai Baba that can help you make this connection with your thoughts: "Before you speak, ask yourself: Is it kind, is it necessary, is it true, does it improve upon the silence?" (A Quote by Sathya Sai Baba, n.d.). You can ask yourself these four questions even before your thoughts become meaningful concepts. Apply this to your thoughts and you would surely see a difference in your thinking pattern. This can be your first practice to shift your mindset and acknowledge the problem.

The subconscious and the conscious mind do not know the difference between negative and positive energy. They just know it as energy. So, they absorb whatever you are focusing on. But if you recognize the negative energies and thoughts immediately, you can nip the negativity in the bud. A little self-criticism is necessary for us to improve our habits and grow as a person. But there is a big difference between "I need to work harder" and "I don't have the caliber, or I am not good enough." Notice your own vocabulary and see what kind of words your brain uses to make sense of the situations around you. Your words (even in your thoughts) matter and you should use them for your betterment instead of downfall. "Death and life are in the power of the tongue; those who love it will eat its fruit" (*Bible Gateway*, 2011, Proverbs 18:21).

Once you determine the tone of your thoughts and shift your mindset (even a little bit goes a long way), you can move forward, and try to face your negative emotions as they come to you because now, they should not cripple you with anxiety or depressive moods. Facing your negativity can be stressful and difficult. It is alright if, for the first few times, you give in to your negative emotions or run away from facing them. Be kind to yourself, and try again. Remind yourself that confrontation will empower you, and you can do it.

So, the next step is what Hal Elrod speaks of in his 5-minute rule. "When upset, spend exactly 5 minutes venting negativity. Feel free to complain, moan, yell or do whatever you need to do. Once the five minutes are over, accept the situation in full. It's impossible to change the past. But you can determine your next steps" (Win at Life, 2015). So, you can allow yourself to feel the pain for five minutes, but then, get up and work on it. We will talk about daily mental exercises you could do to help you in this area later on. No more than five minutes a day should be spent feeling miserable. If you see a beautiful cloud pass over you, you experience the beauty, acknowledge it, and let the cloud pass. You don't keep chasing the cloud. This is how you treat your positive thoughts, don't you? You can do the same with your negative thoughts too, experience their negativity, acknowledge it, and then let it pass.

Our brain is wired in a way that it tries to make sense of the world by creating stories, which are not necessarily the truth, but the best guesses. However, these guesses don't really feel like guesses, they feel like the truth. So, in the end, our interpretation of the world/ourselves creates how we consistently act, feel, or believe. So, question your own narrative and rephrase it. Open up some space in your mind for new narratives. Explore all the alternative ideas of truth. Choose the positive and hopeful stories you want to believe, and only act on them. When we see things only one way, we are rigid and inflexible. So, try to open up to new ideas, thoughts, and experiences however useless they seem at first.

Don't fight your negativity, don't try to resist it. Because in resisting it you'd be focusing on it too much and hence, only thinking about it. Carl Jung said it too, "what you resist not only persists, but grows in size." Pilots know this very well. They are trained to not look at the obstacles in the path, not to give them any value—they just focus on their own path because if they focus on the obstacle, they will surely hit it. They need to allocate their attention to more important and straightforward things. Therefore, understanding your negativity, acknowledging it, and having the courage to not dwell on it, can help you focus on the more positive aspects of your life instead of the negative. So, acknowledge, breathe, release what you do not want, and align with who you really are, and what you really want.

Even after doing all this, if you find yourself unable to deal with your volatility, I suggest you take a hard look at your physical well-being. Sometimes, we can handle our volatility by doing something that is, seemingly, not relatable to our minds at all i.e. proper sleep and nutrition. If you are feeling low, volatile, or cranky towards the end of the day, notice what you have been eating all day and keep your nutrition in check. If you feel bad just after waking up in the morning, check your sleep cycle. Also, see if you are physically well and not suffering from any ailment, or aches. You can only focus on training your mind if your body is working in optimum condition. Yes, when you're dealing with grief and/or depression, it might seem useless to take care of the body. You might not even think about it as you just want the day to get over. However, you should not just survive the day, you should enjoy it and look forward to the next day. Try eating three proper meals a day, breakfast full of fats and carbs (no sugar), and normal nutritious lunch and dinner along with fruits and veggies. Sometimes, we can be cranky because we don't have the energy to think through our difficult situations. Being "hangry" is not just a joke, it is real, and it can affect your mental cognitive behavior. So, eating right, eating enough, and resting well is first and foremost for your mind to work for you instead of against you.

After checking in with your body, sleep cycle, and nutrition, come back to your mind and your thought patterns. Why and when do you get angry/sad/anxious? When does it usually happen and how often does it happen? Make a diary if you want and keep a check on that data. I have created an example for you to help you start. You should log these details multiple times during the day, if you can:

Thinking About Suicide?

Headings	Date and Time	Sleep Cycle	Nutrition	Feelings
Example	Jan 9th, 8 am	6.5 hours	No breakfast yet. Just coffee	Anxious about deadline

Religiously log in the details and notice when any patterns start emerging. What was that one, or multiple events in your life that brought you to live your life in this way? Was it the death of a loved one, an unsuccessful career, injustice done to you, all the sacrifices you made, or the loss of a relationship? Identify the real-life situation that created the negative environment in your brain. Then, move to your emotions. Try to keep a mental note of what kind of thoughts or situations lead to an anxiety attack, or a bout of depressive loss of energy, or an outburst of anger, or a feeling of worthlessness. How and why did these problems intensify? Identify and define the problem that made you go down this insufferable path. Keep them in mind and face them with an open heart. Fighting a known enemy is better than fighting an unknown one. So, when you get to the bottom of your problem and your pain, you can start taking steps to improve your life, and do all the things you let go of during your depressive state.

Maybe the trigger event was not the start of your depression, but just the starting point of all the devastating events that happened in your life afterward. For instance, you might have lost a job that put a halt to your ten years' worth of effort. You would obviously be disappointed, even angry. And then it was followed by an ugly divorce, which was then followed by an Appendicitis diagnosis. You must think that you are unlucky, helpless, not good enough, lonely, and sad. But look at it this way, maybe all the things that followed your job loss happened because of that imbalance in your career. It might be the major catalyst of all your problems, it might have changed your self-talk into a negative one, which might have affected your relationships. Then your loneliness might have led you to believe you were not good enough, and that's why you did not care for your body and health, which led to your diagnosis. Now, ask this hypothetical version of you—why do you want to commit suicide; to show anger, to end your frustrations and loneliness, to have a sense of control over your life, or to punish yourself? So, what we are doing here is going back to square one, accepting the mishap, and moving on to finding solutions instead. No matter what has happened in your life, or what mistakes you have made in your career or relationships, you still deserve a good life. You should not feel ashamed of seeking a good life and you must not feel alone in your struggle. If you look in the right direction, you will always find help and companionship.

You're not Alone

"Why me?" Have you ever questioned your fate about why it chose you to give all the suffering to? Or have you asked your god "why me" as you have been good and kind this whole time, and it has still happened to you? It is natural for us to feel this way when we go through all the trials and tribulations life throws at us. Especially, when we have been good and hardworking, the suffering becomes insufferable. But I am here to tell you that whatever happened to you, or whatever/whoever you lost, the unfortunate event is not as important as your response to it.

Let me share a story with you: You must have heard about the famous tennis player Arthur Ashe. He won Wimbledon, Australian Open, French Open, and many other tournaments in his lifetime. But his success and good fortune were obstructed when he had his heart bypass surgery. During his surgery, he contracted AIDS because of a blood transfusion. When the public and his fans got to know about the unfortunate news, he was showered with hundreds of letters from fans. They all conveyed their condolences. However, there was one young boy who wrote him a somewhat unique letter. The boy said that whenever he would get the chance, he would ask God why he chose Arthur Ashe to suffer an incurable disease like this. Arthur's reply to this letter was beautiful. He said (Botes, 2017):

> 50 Million children wanted to play Tennis, 5 Million learned to play Tennis, 500,000 learned Professional Tennis, 50 Thousand came to Circuit, 5 Thousand reached the Grand Slam, 50 reached Wimbledon, 4 reached the Semifinals, 2 reached the Finals and I won the cup. When I was holding the cup in my hand, I never asked God: 'Why Me?' So now that I'm in pain, how can I ask God: 'Why Me?'

This is life! Full of ups and downs. While we cannot control what happens to us, we can control what we do about it. This might seem a little counterproductive, especially when we just finished talking about defining your problem and recognizing your pain. However, recognition does not necessarily mean significance. So, when you have defined the problem and confronted your pain, try not to focus on the problem but only on the solution. Looking towards your next step should be your next step.

Moreover, if you still feel that your pain is the greatest of all and that your life has been unjust, please know that you are not alone in facing such situations. I am not denying your pain, I know it can be difficult to even get out of your bed when you are in such pain, but you need to remind yourself that you are not the only one suffering. "Approximately 280 million people in the world have depression… Over 700 000 people die due to suicide every year. Suicide is the fourth leading cause of death in 15-29-year-olds" (World Health Organization, 2021). So many people are suffering from a similar amount of pain. Would you imagine telling these people to commit suicide as you have been telling yourself? Would you suggest suicide to a depressed 15-year-old who has not even had a chance to experience life yet? Your pain is understandable, but your thoughts about ending it all cannot be justified.

Moreover, even if you feel that you would not be able to come out of depression because your pain is too strong, or deep-rooted in your emotions, please remember that your depression does affect your feelings/emotions, but it is not about them at all. Depression is purely clinical. It is caused because of genetic dispositions and is composed of chemical imbalances in the brain. It is a disease that can be cured if you ask for help. Help is always available, you just need to ask for it and not overthink it.

Seek Solution but not Self-Harm

"It's the tolerance and acceptance of the negative experiences that pave the path to positive experiences" (Manson, 2021). You must follow and practice each chapter's suggestions as you keep progressing in the book. Don't procrastinate, you must start right now to see results as soon as possible and initiate this new chapter in your life. You must learn that your pain is just a chemical imbalance that can be balanced with some changes in your perspective. You must know that you are not alone in your pain, so many people suffer from it in the world and most of them recover from it. Your pain is not permanent. You must start going back to the root of this pain, define the problem that led you to be this negative, and accept to yourself that it is perfectly normal for you to feel these emotions and there should be no guilt or shame in being depressed.

Guilt and shame are nothing but social constructs. What should matter to you is your life, your happiness, and your self-worth. So, don't be afraid to ask for help. Confess it to yourself, share it with a close friend and if need be, reach a medical professional. Sometimes confronting your past or your pain is as simple as sitting down with a trusted person and talking to them about it.

When you have seen the lowest that your negativity can take you, the only thing left for you to do is fight it and go back up to your positive self. Accept your pain and learn to tolerate it, at least for a little more time; just until you finish reading this book and applying the tools and exercises I suggest here to your life. You are way too strong to succumb to the seemingly easy solution of ending everything.

Important Details to Remember

1. Confrontation will empower you.
2. Experience your negativity, acknowledge it and then let it pass.
3. Check in with your body, sleep cycle, and nutrition.
4. Keeping a log of your thought patterns can help you recognize the source of your pain.
5. Depression is purely clinical. You can treat it just like any other disease.
6. Sometimes confronting your past or your pain is as simple as sitting down with a trusted person and talking to them about it. Reach out and you will always find help.

CHAPTER 2: KNOW HOW NOT TO GIVE A F*CK

As we discussed in the previous chapter, our minds constantly keep running and absorbing the world around us, including the positive and the negative. If you have already followed the previous chapter, you would have taken control of your self-talk a little bit. But what if it is not you who is the negative talker? People around us influence our thought processes too. What if their negativity is bringing you further down? To tackle others' negativity and stay away from it, we must know how not to give a f*ck.

There are all kinds of people around us. Sometimes strangers act like family and family act like enemies. You cannot take responsibility for handling others' behaviors or negativity. You have to take special care of your headspace when you are already feeling depressed and suicidal and for that, you must stay away from people who do not take your depression seriously while crying about their lower back aches. Do you think these kinds of people have a better outlook on life than you? Do you think you can trust their opinions? Absolutely not. You are the only one who knows how it feels in your skin. So, whatever others say simply does not matter. Politely close the conversation with such people, try to avoid them, and if you can, completely cut them off from your life. You must adopt an "I don't give a f*ck" mentality and create huge opaque walls between you and the toxic people who drain you of your hopefulness and joy.

Moreover, even when you learn to disregard unsolicited opinions and advice gracefully, you might still need to work more on yourself to completely block their negativity. You can do that by improving and solidifying your own sense of being. To reiterate, you must not fixate on the problem. You must not think about pursuing a better life desperately, as pursuing it would only mean that you lack it right now. So, do not fixate on your end goal but try and opt for moderation in your feelings, your thoughts, and your goals. Of course, maintaining distance from toxic/negative people is important but moderation is the key to not giving a f*ck.

The Golden Mean theory by Aristotle is one of the most rational things that you can follow to achieve moderation, which simply asks you to adopt a middle way. But still, in practice, it becomes difficult for us to understand how much is too much and how much is too little. This was originally theorized to tell people how to be virtuous (morally) but this can be applied to so many other things as well. However, Aristotle does not mention any set of rules or any ways to tell you what to do exactly. The only way to learn it is through experience and good judgment. You just need to find a midpoint between extremes, for instance, you should be somewhere between extreme blissfulness and extreme despair. Or you should have enough courage to not be a coward but also know better than to be reckless. You will have some more clarity through this table:

Too Much	The Golden Mean	Too Little
Wasteful Extravagance	Generosity	Stinginess
Religious Asceticism	Moderate Self Restraint	Worldly Self Indulgence
Elation	Contentment	Depression
Order	Explorative Possibilities	Chaos
Immortality	Being and Existence	Death

I always keep repeating this saying to my daughter—Not too much, not too little, in the middle. A balanced life is the key to a healthy life. Clearly, this principle is not just for a healthy life, you must have this balance to be able to not care about the unproductive and toxic environment as well. Try to find contentment in life. Don't focus your time working on the past or the future. Live in the moment, seek the now. Also, you should have a strong and secure sense of self by honing your strengths while working on your weaknesses. Let me guide you on how to achieve it.

You Are Imperfect but Still Valuable

Do you think you are valuable to society or to anyone? Do you feel that had you attained that perfect life or that six-figure salary, your value would have increased? Are you equating success in your career to the value of your life? Or do you believe you are not valuable because someone abuses you and tells you the same? Do you think you have to look a certain way? Or are you trying to have the perfect family you always wanted? We have always been told by society and social media that a successful person has a great job, six figures salary, and a great loving family. That is how our minds have been shaped and even manipulated to believe in something that is not necessarily true. Your definition of success is yours alone and you should not compare yourself to anybody else because you don't have to live somebody else's dream life. Your birth in your family, the people around you, and your experiences in your life make you unique. Therefore, if someone else has a perfect marriage, a luxurious house, and a car, you might be attracted to that life but there is no guarantee that it will make you happy. So, if you have a definition of your perfect life or successful life, I am here to change it so that you learn to care a little less for these societal constructs.

Life is ever evolving and changing. There is simply not enough time for life to stand still and attain perfection. Therefore, all life is beautiful but imperfect. Perfection itself is imperfect. Nothing is absolute and our life will always have room for improvement or would just run its course in due time. So, it's futile running after the perfect life, or even the happiest self. You can ask for fulfillment, and you can ask for satisfaction, but you should not run after perfection. Because perfection would not be the middle way. Try and tell yourself that life is always going to be imperfect, as it is for almost each and every human being on this earth. Life is imperfect for all, it is imperfect for Elon Musk, Brad Pitt, and even the President of the United States. Life will always have room for advancement and maybe even greater attainment. This imperfection of life exists mostly because we, too, are forever changing and growing beings. We wanted different things in life when we were teenagers, and we might want something completely different in our thirties. So, neither should we run after a perfect life nor towards a perfect self, because none of those exists.

Now that we have established the insignificance of perfection, we can safely say that even if things didn't turn out to be perfect, you don't have to care about it at all. That's the way it is! You can just accept the failure and move forward, toward something else that might work out for you. It can be difficult to accept defeat and even more difficult to move on. That is exactly why most of us have this "all or nothing" attitude ingrained in us. For instance, suppose Martha was recently told by the doctor to lower her cholesterol levels, take care of her diet and only eat home-cooked meals every day. But if by any chance, she ate even a bite of unhealthy or junk food, her resolutions would lapse and she would go back to her old "gorging on fast food" cycle. Her mind said that if she had already ruined her diet because of this slip-up, she might as well eat till her stomach hurts. This is a dangerous attitude to have because it essentially means that Martha is avoiding responsibility for her failure. She did not want to accept her failure of keeping her diet in check, so slipped even more and blamed it on the unfortunate time that her partner offered her a bite from his cheeseburger. This attitude does not just make us avoid responsibility for our failure, but in the long run, creates a fear of failure in our minds, and this fear turns our world upside down by making us anxious and stressed all the time. This fear makes us believe that maybe we are not good enough to follow through.

These little slip-ups and failures are ostensibly the success deterrent activities that every one of us should avoid being successful. However, this is not true. You can be successful even after doing all these seemingly wrong things. Your success is only determined by your efforts. Your efforts should always be 100%. All the rest of the mistakes, slip-ups, and overthinking should be secondary. Focusing too much on the outcome will keep you from giving your 100 percent but not thinking about the task at hand will also keep you from giving your 100 percent. So, besides the task at hand, you should not give a f*ck to anything or anyone. Overthinking about Martha's slip-up kept her from giving her 100 percent to her diet. Had she just taken a bite and brought herself back to performing at 100 percent effort, she would not have eaten so much the rest of the day. This 100 percent effort too, can be achieved only when you are neither underperforming nor overperforming. Because either of those things would make you think more and do less. So, here too, we must keep the Golden Mean Theory in mind.

So, your imperfections do not dictate your value and neither does your success. You should honor your efforts, withdraw your energy and attention from what society wants you to do, and reconnect with yourself. Don't seek your value from outside, as that's how we let others manipulate us to get their approval which we only get when we do their bidding. Making others happy is not our job. Your value does not come from what you do for others, what you accomplish in life, or how much money you earn. You are valuable because you are the only one in the history of humankind who is just like you, with your opinions, knowledge, experiences, and values. You are unique and you were born for a reason. Your existence on this earth gives you the title of being invaluable, however imperfect you might think you are. You do not need to push yourself to extremes to prove your worth. Think to yourself that even if you are not better than everyone else around you, you are surely just as valuable and just as good.

You have all the ability to achieve what you want to, leave a legacy, and live the life you want to live. Even if you do not achieve it, I am here to tell you that you are still valuable and loved. Ideals created by society are not the measure of your value; your slip-ups and failures are not the measures of your value. It's your effort, your ability to love, and your strong sense of self that brings value to the world. You bring value to your spouse, your parents, your children, and your friends by just being in their lives and by just spending time with them.

In the end, you must be comfortable with your identity even if it's different from others or different from what you hoped it would be. When you achieve satisfaction in being in your own skin, you will have a very strong sense of self and would never give a f*ck about what others think or say because you would be sure about the things that really matter.

Know What Triggers You

So, you are imperfect as is everybody else. Also, you are unspecial just like everyone else is. You must be thinking how can I say that no one is special? Our parents always said that we all are special, but what they actually wanted to say was that we are special to them. However, in the world, all human beings stand on the same pedestal. So many people are living their lives like you are, worrying like you are, or maybe even thinking about suicide. Almost everyone suffers in life. So their comments or judgments are, in reality, a mirror reflecting their own insecurities. They might be depressed too, or frustrated with life. I am not invalidating your emotions but trying to give you a different perspective that everyone who comments/judges you, worries about being judged themselves. You should never dwell on it because it does not align with your goals. Even if people are dragging you through the mud, it depends on you if you consider it an insult or not. We are in charge of our own emotions. You must not give anyone else the power to control your feelings.

We already talked about how we can handle our pain and our volatile emotions. We learned to recognize our emotions and change how we react to those emotions by being in control. However, our impulses and emotions can be unpredictable and quite dependent on outside factors. If you find someone or something that triggers negative emotions, you should follow the five minutes rule, recognize where and why it hurts, and then forget about it. Once you do this, you can start working on the efforts in the direction of your goals. Leave the emotion and act on your goals. So, if Martha, who is struggling herself with her crash diets and inability to follow through, comments on how fat you look, you can feel shitty about yourself for some time, let it go, and then re-align your thoughts to your goals. This is the first step towards not giving a f*ck. When you keep following this, you would notice that you would no longer need the five minutes to feel and let go of your negative emotions. You would straightaway ignore the useless information/comment and move towards something more productive. "There is a huge amount of freedom that comes to you when you take nothing personally" (Borchard, 2015). So, when it comes to not caring, you don't always have to align your thoughts with your actions. Actually, your actions are the quickest way to change your thoughts. So, focus on actions and efforts you can make in the present and let your negative go.

Protecting Your Headspace by Learning to Say "No"

Now you know that no matter what has happened in your life, you are still valuable. You have also learned that no comment/judgment from others can affect your value or emotions. But sometimes, even after knowing all possible things about stress, anxiety, and our own values, we still find it difficult to deal with them. You might have been told many times "You should not be stressed," "why are you so stressed about such menial things," or even when people know we are stressed, all they can come up with is "don't be stressed." No matter how much we google our chronic stress symptoms or anxiety treatments at home, we cannot seem to apply this abundantly available knowledge to ourselves. We still worry about the little things and waste our strength on them. It is all about not being able to control what goes on in our lives. Internally, we have learned to keep our emotions in check. However, there is one external thing as well, that we can control—our time.

Our joy in life comes from doing the activities we love doing. Whether it is spending quality family time, going to a new restaurant, or watching a film, we all have some activities that we love doing. However, once we stop doing these activities, our joy keeps fading away. We turn sour and cranky. We start hating the things that never really bothered us earlier. All because we did not take out any time for our joy to flourish. Maybe it was because of too much workload in the office, or the never-ending chores at home, it might even be because of the goodness of our hearts as we keep on caring about others and forgetting about ourselves. We say yes to almost anything a family member or friend asks. We keep on doing somebody else's work for them or worse, we keep on doing all the work by ourselves without asking for help. All these activities are sucking the joy out of you. You need to be in control of your time.

The first thing you can do to gain more control is to change your body language. We know that our confident and powerful-looking body language can influence others. But surprisingly these non-verbal can even influence how we think and perceive ourselves. So, whenever you are talking to someone who takes away your joy, consciously try to stand in the Superwoman Pose with a straight spine. Or any other pose that makes you take up more space than usual, with your arms open or on your waist with a straight spine and even a puffed-up chest. You might see a difference in your tone and a little more confidence boost to say "No" to whatever does not make you happy.

If our work, relationship, or hobbies are not giving us joy, we must learn to say "No" to those activities. Moreover, "No" can give you peace by providing you with the power to take care of your own interests instead of just pleasing people and then feeling miserable later. So, next time someone asks you for a favor that will impact your joy negatively, you must politely decline the request. However, this does not mean that you should not help anyone at all, and only care about your "me time." All you need to do is ask yourself, will doing this favor bring me joy? Is this my responsibility? Am I the only person who can do this? The Bible teaches us to be compassionate, helpful, and self-sacrificing but it never says to keep on helping others to the point it becomes detrimental to you.

I understand when our feelings get in the way of creating boundaries. For instance, you and your partner live together and are both working and earning individuals. However, you find yourself preparing all the meals, washing all the dishes, and even doing the laundry, while your partner enjoys reels on Instagram, or long walks in the nearby park. Because of all this work, you are mostly just checking out items from your mental checklist instead of calming yourself with a nice book and a cup of coffee. You love your partner and would do anything for them; however, doing all these chores and not asking for help will prove to be very damaging to your relationship. Because you did not protect your headspace, did not say no, and did not ask for help, you will start resenting your partner. So, you must learn to have enough time and mental headspace in your life to enjoy the little things that bring you joy.

What if a toxic person is part of your family and you have to entertain them from time to time? It would be difficult to say "No" to family gatherings and even worse to pick a fight with this toxic person and ask your family to choose sides. Here, we can create a barrier. If you find that a person triggers you or bothers your headspace, discard them from your life. But if they are close to you already, try to create a wall between you and this person so that his/her toxicity does not pass through the wall and get to you. Keep your conversations light with this person and strictly avoid talking to them about your feelings and emotions.

At last, saying no to others is still easier than saying no to yourself. We must learn to say no to our own minds and thoughts which seem negative. You can do this by taking some cues from chapter one and from the previous section as well. You need to remember that your end goal here is to create a strong sense of self. Once you have a strong sense of self, an understanding of the value of your time on this earth, and a willingness to say "no" to your negative thoughts, you will automatically be able to only care about the important things in life.

Know When and Where to Give a F*ck

We have learned the how(s) and why(s) of not giving a f*ck but we must also know when and where to really do give a f*ck. Obsessing over the past/future, seeking a utopian life, overthinking about a problem you cannot control, people-pleasing, and trying to control everything about your life are all examples of giving a lot of importance to unyielding things. But don't we take ourselves too seriously sometimes, by taking the toxicity from others personally? So, the first thing to do is not to take anything personally, not even your own thoughts. Learn what hurts you the most and shut it off.

Again, remember the Golden Mean Theory and do not obsess over this. Just keep doing the best you can manage and only care about your goals, your ideals, your meaningful relationships, your mental health, your body, and your spirit. When you have a good sense of self and your goals set, you will automatically know when and where to give a f*ck.

Important Details to Remember

1. Create huge opaque walls between you and toxic people.
2. Practice the Golden Mean theory: not too much, not too little, in the middle.
3. Perfect life is just a societal construct and a lie.

4. It's your effort, your ability to love, and your strong sense of self that brings value to the world.
5. You should straightaway ignore the useless information/comment and move towards something more productive.
6. If our work, relationship, or hobbies are not giving us joy, we must learn to say "No" to those activities.
7. Don't take anything personally, not even your own thoughts. Learn what hurts you the most and shut it off.

CHAPTER 3: THE POWER OF FORGIVENESS

It is a sad reality of the world that we live among various kinds of morally ambiguous people. Some people commit crimes against us by abusing us physically or mentally, or by cheating us with either material assets or our trust. Sometimes, in our lowest moments, we commit these morally dubious things ourselves. We all have been hurt by someone, or we might have hurt someone as well. Mistakes are made in almost every relationship and so, forgiveness is always going to be a part of our lives.

The bitterness and the anger that comes along with these wrongs committed against us can be debilitating. It becomes difficult to forgive someone who has left a huge hole in our lives. And similarly, it becomes even more difficult to forgive ourselves if we have been the culprit in ruining someone else's life. It wears away your confidence.

However, cursing someone else or feeling guilty the whole time can make you very stressed, and can even cause anxiety attacks. It would always feel like debt is owed from the culprit to the victim. Maybe you want to get even with them. But these feelings will only hurt you and no one else. If you continue holding a grudge, you will never be able to free yourself from your unfortunate experience.

Your anger towards the perpetrator will never affect them but only you. The longer you feed the anger and the bitterness, the more hold the perpetrator will have on you. That is the opposite of what we want. We want peace, happiness and fulfillment that we can only attain once we let go of this poison that we keep ingesting willingly. Do not let your negative emotions get a hold of you. Read on to find out how.

Why the Grudge?

Have you been thinking about your perpetrator more than anything else? Do you feel that something is affecting your relationship with others, and yourself? Do you feel emotionally exhausted because of a grudge you hold?

Firstly, let us logically address these feelings. I think you will agree when I say that we human beings have free will, and we choose how to act on that free will. As your perpetrator chose to act immorally, holding a grudge against them is also a choice of action. You might even believe in God and feel that this injustice/evil was done to you by God's consent. But if God is good, then there must be a reason behind all that happened. The most probable reason can only be God intending you to learn from the experience. Moreover, we can be sure about one thing—God, for sure, does not want you to hold a grudge, as only he has the wisdom and the authority to judge someone, and be angry with them. Our grudge has neither any purpose nor productivity if we place our trust in God.

I believe that you know this logic too, and still find it hard to let go of the anger. I understand it is not as easy as it sounds. Let me give you another logical explanation for this: Human beings, while capable of intelligent and sustainable development of themselves, usually face hurdles in doing so because of their biases. It is in our nature to think of things in counter position which always directs us to look at the negatives. So how do we fight our instincts?

According to Burns (2009), we need something strong that can appeal to our will, our intellect and our sensitivity to open ourselves to push forward. Therefore, what we need is faith, hope and love that can appeal to all three of our characteristics respectively. So, practice all the activities that indulge faith, hope and love every day. Pray, meditate, visualize a positive future where you have no baggage of your grudges, commit acts of charity out of love and practice self-love every day. This can lay the foundation and can direct you to forgiveness and the freedom that comes with it.

On another note, we also know that we must act against evil, and our inaction means that we are a part of it. So, you must act to fight this evil you are committing against yourself. Your active participation is necessary to get rid of the grudge because your grudge is making you mentally and maybe even physically ill, and you are amplifying this by not letting it go. Your suppressed anger and bitterness cause your stress levels to elevate, and your elevated stress levels can cause gut problems and even pose a risk to your cardiovascular health. So, holding a grudge can be equivalent to self-harm.

By letting go of a grudge you will, by no means, be trying to bring about a change in your perpetrator. You neither need to reconcile with them. All you need to do is stop thinking and being angry about the unfortunate event that vexes you. Try to look for the best in people and have some altruism at the back of your mind because if you don't, you would even find faults in God. "Without faith... the world is too evil for God to be good" (Lonergan, 2003, p.117). It does not matter which faith you have or what philosophy you believe in, what matters is your complete trust in the goodness of the world. When you recognize the inherent good, even in unscrupulous actions, then you will never even hold a grudge in the first place.

The other significant reason that we hold a grudge against someone is our ego. We all have an ego that relates closely to our self-esteem and pride. It is most natural for anyone to hold a grudge against someone who has hurt their pride. Whether it was a conscious decision of theirs to hurt us or unconscious, does not matter, what matters is how we take it. We have talked about it already in the previous chapter that we must not take anything personally however, that was the case of not giving a f*ck. On the other hand, we hold a grudge against someone not just because they said something hurtful but because they hurt us through their actions. If someone else's actions make us feel small and insignificant, we will hold a grudge against them and be angry at them. How can we divert this whole situation? We know we cannot control someone else's actions, the only thing we can control here is how we perceive ourselves and if it really does align with what the perpetrator said about us. The best way to approach this is to adopt a method that stoicism suggests we do i.e. adopting the cosmic viewpoint. Plato called it the Bird's Eye View.

All you need to do is introspect. Sit by yourself in a calm room and close your eyes. Imagine yourself as a bird who is sitting on the fan above you and looking at you sitting. Then zoom out even further and look at yourself through the roof, and then zoom out more and look at the smallness of your house/apartment. Keep on zooming out till you imagine yourself looking at yourself from the outer atmosphere of the earth. The whole point of this exercise is to reduce your troubles' value in your eyes. The whole world is so big and so varied. There is always something going on and something that one has to do. When you train your perception this way regularly, you will reduce your pride to something that only you appreciate. This does not mean you should devalue yourself, on the contrary, this clarifies how much value you actually have because just like your troubles seem insignificant from the Bird's Eye View, your culprit's actions against you are even smaller. It will tell you how your culprit's wrongdoings can never be substantial enough to be of any consequence in the world. Their attack on your self-esteem/pride is not significant, as they do not know a single thing about your pride. That is something only you can fathom, without expecting anyone else to measure it for you.

Therefore, try to introspect more so that you never hold a grudge against someone in the future because all it does is make you bitter and angry all the time. It takes away your joy and gives you stress. It acts like a heavy backpack that you have to carry constantly. Don't hold a grudge and experience the freedom of never lifting that backpack again. These introspections can also lay a foundation for you to be more forgiving and flexible.

Trust the Process and Be Patient

Let us list some ways you can start your forgiveness process. We will discuss some practical strategies that will help change your perspective and also some hands-on tools you can use to bring about a change. Let us use John Doe as our perpetrator's name to make things easier.

1. **Analyze the offense:** Did John Doe mentally abuse you, or physically hurt you? Or was the offense a hurtful comment, a deception, a lie, or a breaking of trust? Define what hurt you the most and analyze why it did.

2. **Talk to John Doe:** You should only think about doing it if you are comfortable enough with them. There is no need for you to do this if it is making you anxious or worried. Also, this does not apply to your abuser but only to your close friends/family who have hurt you sentimentally. So, if you are comfortable talking about it, try to sit with John and calmly explain what he did to hurt you, why you feel hurt and how you wish it had not been done. And also admit where you went wrong in the whole situation. Talk compassionately and see how it

goes. If you instantly get a genuine apology, you would automatically know that all of it was maybe a mistake. However, if you don't, no worries. At least you'll know you tried to clear things up. And this process did make it clear for you whether this person is worth keeping in your life, or not.

3. **Forgiving can never mean forgetting:** You must not consider your talk with John as a way of forgetting everything and moving on. For your own happiness and self-respect's sake, do not give anyone the chance to hurt you repeatedly. If they have hurt you once, most likely your relationship with them will change for good. It should always be your conscious decision whether you want to continue your relationship as before, or if you want to maintain some distance. Especially, in the case of heinous crimes done against you, I would suggest you let go but never forget the wrong. The purpose of forgiveness is to free your mind from the baggage of your grudge/anger, and not ignore the wrongs or pardon them because forgetting them would make you available, yet again, to be used/cheated/hurt and doing that would not be a very prudent

decision. Always remember that our relationships are as fragile as a thread and once broken, things will automatically change, and even if they are mended again, they will always have a knot that no one can really get rid of.

4. **Realize that it is NOT your responsibility to change John:** No matter how many times you forgive them, some people never change. Taking care of their actions is their responsibility, no matter how much you want to influence them to change. So your responsibility is just to get rid of John's negativity from your mind, forgive him and move on. Never expect anything in return and never try to change John. You have so many more important things to do.

5. **Remember the time when you hurt someone:** Keep on reminding yourself of an incident where you committed a mistake and the other one forgave you for it. Remember how it felt to be in the shoes of the culprit. Maybe you felt guilty or shameful. John might be feeling the same. Maybe this would help make you a little less angry and a little more forgiving.

You must practice these five suggestions and see how much difference it makes. It is possible that your wound is quite fresh and so, it is difficult for you to even think about forgiveness right now. In this scenario, give it some time. However, do not just sit around during this time thinking that time would heal you. Sometimes it does, but most of the time it does not. We just gain the right perspective after some time, that's what brings about the change.

So, if you are giving yourself some time before you think about forgiving John, keep on practicing two things in your daily life so that the process of forgiveness becomes easier for you later. Firstly, keep on practicing empathy, not just in the case of John, but in general. Try to empathize with your spouse, your children or your siblings. Try to understand their point of view and make it a habit of knowing others' side of the story as well.

Another practice that you must follow is to decide to forgive consciously. Make it a point to forgive all the little mishaps or rude people you encounter every day. This practice can especially help if you are trying to take some time to get used to the idea of forgiveness, or when you feel way too angry/negative to be in the right head to forgive. It will take time but slowly your negative wishes for John would change to either no wishes, or positive ones. You can learn to do that by forgiving the less intensive and everyday events, like someone cutting you in line, or someone talking to you rudely. Recognize that you feel angry, try being in the shoes of the other person (maybe it wasn't personal), and then let it go to forgive them right there and then. If you keep on practicing conscious forgiveness everyday, maybe later you can decide to forgive even more intense wrongs done to you.

On the contrary, if you feel that you are the one who has wronged someone else and you find it difficult to forgive yourself for it, please allow yourself to be vulnerable about your feelings towards the person you have wronged. Apologize to them and tell them how much you care. Let the other person judge you however they want to, let them yell at you and show them that you know you are at fault. Then approach them from time to time and portray yourself to be a trustworthy person so that they can trust you again. Lastly and most importantly, give them time to process the situation and later forgive you.

However, if you do all the above steps to make things right and they still did not forgive you, you must learn to move on from it too. If you genuinely followed all the above-suggested steps, then it is all that you can do to make things right. Then, the ball is in their court. If they decide to not let go, they must come to terms with the situation on their own. You, on the other hand, have no control over it and therefore, there is no point in fussing over their decision. Our goal here is to heal ourselves and do the right thing. Anything more than that would be unproductive.

In the end, being a forgiving person is a long and difficult process where you need to constantly work on your thoughts, feelings, and actions simultaneously. To be forgiving and free of the extra burden that you have been carrying all this while, you need to have self-awareness and a will to transform. If you have these two, following the steps and being consistent would be easier for you, and healing will come to you sooner. Even if you do not have these qualities right now, I am sure by the end of reading this chapter and practicing it, you will acquire them. This process is yours and the end result would be yours to enjoy as well, so the timeline should be according to you too. Don't worry about the timeline, just keep on working on yourself and trust the process.

Heal Through Forgiveness

Now, you know about all the logical explanations for why forgiveness is necessary and all the steps you need to achieve it. The next step is to heal through this whole experience of forgiveness. Healing can look and feel different to everybody so, you would have to try multiple things and know which one brings you the most peace and the most joy. Also, healing will always be a meaningful personal transformation. So keep your mind and heart open to new methodologies. Let us look at some of the tips that can help you heal through forgiveness.

In the process of forgiving our perpetrators, we discussed above that we need to check once if our perpetrators consciously tried to hurt us or not, and create boundaries in case we would not be able to trust them again. But forgiveness is about healing not about creating walls around yourself. So, keep in mind that setting boundaries and creating emotional walls around yourself are two completely different things and we must never merge them together. Try to adopt setting boundaries and discard the constant emotional walls, this is what we want to achieve. If we are trying to heal ourselves, our healed personality should be able to express ourselves freely and authentically. To bring this kind of energy and healing into our lives, we would have to be self-compassionate, transpersonal, and a little spiritual.

Most of the time when we are hurting from previous trauma, we end up behaving in an escapist manner. We want to numb ourselves, so that we don't feel the things we desperately need to feel, to heal. So, we start escaping our feelings by drinking more, smoking more, having multiple sexual partners, or over-eating, and sometimes we even tend to oversleep. This is a normal response to trauma, as you are trying to save yourself from the stress of it all through these activities. This is nothing but further self-harm. Escapism is the easy way but not the right way. We have to be with our pain face to face. For healing to start, we must consciously think about our trauma daily. This exercise can be your savior. Think about how it was carried out, think about who did it and essentially relive it. It will hurt and I understand if you cannot bring yourself to do this every day. However, there is no other method, someday or the other you would have to face your trauma and it would be better if you start it as soon as possible. Narrate the unfortunate incident to yourself, ask yourself which parts hurt the most, and what you learned about yourself from this experience. Relive your trauma again and again, and every day (if possible). When you think about it and relive it this much, its value would start depleting, and your future self's value would increase. It would not feel as painful as it did earlier. When it stops being so painful, you can further progress toward self-love as a part of your healing. You can do all the things that bring you joy and happiness. You can treat yourself to a good cup of tea/coffee, or you can go for a spa treatment, or you could go on a holiday with the people you love the most. So, to bring yourself to forgive your culprit, you must go through this two-step process of reliving your trauma repeatedly and practicing self-love to make up for the pain you put yourself through.

Moreover, to heal through forgiveness you have to transcend to a place without your ego. Just as we talked about in the previous section, you must practice the Bird's Eye View for you to leave behind your ego and have a wider perspective that includes not just yourself and your perpetrator but the whole wide world and its suffering. When you leave behind your ego and gain a wider perspective, you will see that forgiveness is beyond giving and receiving. Your forgiveness is neither for you to give to someone nor for you to take from someone. It is a transformational process for your inner self where you let go of your pain and anger. You must transcend yourself first to gain this perspective and be one with the whole world to validate your perspective. There is another way to achieve this—through spirituality.

Spirituality can hugely affect our ability to forgive and is the most powerful process to achieve healing. If you are religious, then religion can help you in the exact same manner. It will force you to look inward and urge you to transform for the better. The main methodology to achieve this is meditation or praying, whichever you feel most comfortable doing. Try to do this alone in a peaceful place, where you would not be disturbed. While meditating or praying, think of your perpetrator and yourself. Try to open up to feel the unconditional love of God and the world, in general. You, just like God, have this capability to love unconditionally as well as forgive any wrong done to you. A research study that included psychological, theological, and philosophical perspectives on forgiveness concluded that through meditation, spiritual connection, and/or religion, multiple people found a way to extend their egos and embody a mystical transcendence that was beyond anger and pain (Mihalache, 2009). These people included ones who had lost their loved ones in 9/11, ones who suffered domestic abuse, rape victims, and even survivors of the Holocaust. They all followed different religions and ethnic backgrounds ranging from Buddhism, Taoism, and Vedanta to Christianity, Judaism, and Native American paganism. They all started their spiritual practices with the intent of regulating their emotions, and achieving some solace. However, they came out of their journey with a new transcendental discovery of forgiveness. One of the participants, Azim, lost his son to a violent shooting. He shared his own story of forgiveness for Mihalache's research study (2009):

> I felt my own life force draining out of me from my head to my toes. And with the pain too great to bear, I had the spiritual experience of leaving my body. In this altered state of consciousness, I felt held and comforted in the arms of my God. There, in that state of peace, I realized a profound truth, simply this: there were

victims at both ends of the gun. Through forgiveness, I went from a tough international investment banker to a healer. This has been a blessing and a miracle in my life and continues to provide me with solace, peace, and meaning on an ongoing basis. The biggest gift my son gave to me is that through his death I was kicked onto my path of teaching forgiveness, the path of my foundation, the path of stopping children from killing children. When you're on path, it is amazing how the Universe supports you. This is what makes this story both a tragedy and a blessing... It is truly a circle of love moving out, coming back, and moving out again. As other people heal, I heal further. My story shows that something meaningful can come from something meaningless. (p. 125, 127)

Therefore, you must try to adopt a spiritual and/or religious practice that resonates the most with you. You can even try guided meditations to initiate your journey.

Forgiveness can prove to be nothing less than a blessing when achieved after a long struggle. You deserve to experience this kind of magical and surreal peacefulness. You owe it to yourself to make this happen in your life.

When you do, I am positive that you will thank yourself later and continue following these practices.

Important Details to Remember

1. Your anger towards the perpetrator will never affect them but only you.
2. As your perpetrator chose to act immorally, holding a grudge against them is also a choice of action.
3. We need faith, hope, and love to open ourselves to forgiveness.
4. Recognize the inherent good, even in unscrupulous actions, to spare yourself from holding a grudge in the future.
5. Practice the "Bird's Eye View" to know how your culprit's wrongdoings can never be substantial enough, to be of any consequence in the world.
6. Techniques to practice forgiveness: Analyze the offense, talk to your perpetrator, forgive but don't forget, realize that changing your perpetrator is not your responsibility, and remember the time when you hurt someone.

7. Your forgiveness is neither for you to give to someone nor for you to take from someone. It is a transformational process for your inner self where you let go of your pain and anger.
8. You must try to adopt a spiritual and/or religious practice that resonates the most with you, to help you with forgiveness.

CHAPTER 4: GRATITUDE INVENTORY

Every year, the whole United States sits together at the table and celebrates Thanksgiving, with a plate full of Turkey. We love the holiday, but seldom for the right reasons. The tradition is quite old and has been followed for many years; however, the sentiment should still be the same. Thanksgiving as the name suggests is all about gratitude. While it is great that we have a whole festival based on this brilliant virtue, it also makes many people uncomfortable. Thanking your friends/family/God for all your gifts the previous year can only be done if you have a tranquil heart. It becomes difficult to thank someone when you shy away from being open about your feelings in front of them, or when you do not even feel very grateful in the first place. Of course, it would be uncomfortable to thank someone if you are not genuinely grateful, or if you feel entitled to all the good things in your life. You might even feel sad during this time, as you might think that you have no one to thank, and nothing to be grateful for in life. Of course, this is not the right perspective.

This holiday is the most important one because it teaches us the most critical thing—to be happy in our lives. Isn't happiness what you are searching for? This chapter is the most vital one for you in this case, as gratitude is the most widely researched and confirmed trait of all happy people. It is said to be a character trait of all the fighters who have gone through some of the most difficult times in life and have still found their happiness. Most of the depression survivors claim that it was their gratitude that brought them out of the darkness, and led them into the light. So, it becomes imperative for us to learn this skill, and move one step closer to our aim of being happy and content in our lives.

Gratitude is simply the acknowledgment and recognition of something valuable given to us free of cost. It is more than just a feeling, it is a deep emotional response to an act of goodness done to us. For instance, I can be grateful for my spouse's unconditional love and support. It simply means that I cherish and appreciate my partner's actions, which she/he is giving to me without asking for anything in return.

I feel blessed to have this gift from them, and always feel warm when she/he showers me with this gift. This is not a fleeting feeling but a very deep and warm emotion that keeps coming back to me. This is what gratitude feels like. It is a beautiful sentiment and vocalizing this sentiment can let others feel it too.

Gratitude can fill you with positivity and can touch others positively too. If you train yourself to gravitate more toward this emotion, you will start having stronger and closer relationships, you will start seeing improvement in your moods, and feel a hundred times lighter. It will allow you to focus your energy on the goodness that you already have rather than the things you feel you lack. But the road to a gratitude-filled heart is never too easy. We become our own enemies sometimes. However, nothing is impossible with practice and training. Our goal by the end of the chapter would be to change our attitude towards life to a grateful and blessed one.

Obstacles in the Way of Leading a Grateful Life

You are almost halfway through the book, so you must be used to the practice of always recognizing your problems first. We have been doing this since the first chapter. Here too, we must recognize the hindrances that keep us away from being grateful, and then, we must either steer clear of those hindrances or learn to win over them.

Let us address the biggest hindrance that you might be facing right now—your desire to end your life. I believe you are going backward in your previous decision of ending your life, and moving towards hope after reading the previous chapters. However, I understand that you might need something more powerful than hope to sustain you on this path to happiness. The strongest thing that can put a stop to your negativity is gratitude. To achieve it, you must slowly untie all the complex knots in your emotions that are blocking your gratitude, and not letting you recognize the good things you are meant to enjoy. However, it would take a long time for you to achieve the mental peace required to think about what others have done for you, and how you can thank them. Therefore, we can take a shortcut by directly going toward redemption. Let us turn the source of our negativity into the catalyst of our redemption. So, if you have been depressed about your child's recently diagnosed Down's Syndrome (DS), turn this news into the beginning of a great redemption movie script in your mind. Your child's DS does not determine her future, she is still a child with a wide range of emotions and she still loves and depends on you. Maybe your child, if given the right circumstances and support, turns out to be a genius piano player. Her success might be your redemption. Or maybe her unconditional love for you proves to be your redemption.

When you overcome your pain and find redemption, you might be able to feel grateful for all the help you could get in the process. You might be grateful for your daughter's relentless and infectious happiness. You might be grateful for your spouse's constant support.

The other hindrance in your journey towards gratefulness can be your negative biases. We touched upon it in the previous chapter as well. Our minds have a natural tendency to focus more on the negative than the positive because our problem-solving mind always wins over our peaceful minds. So, we might find more faults with people than qualities. In other words, we might not be able to let go of the mistakes they have made previously to acknowledge their good deeds in the present. We can overcome this tendency by practicing forgiveness as we discussed in the previous chapter and by being in the moment. Therefore, even if your boyfriend talked negatively about you behind your back earlier, you must not let yourself even think about his past actions before thanking him for his support while facing your abusive parents. The moment the other person does some good for you without taking anything in return, you must thank them. This is not a regular practice necessarily but just for the cases when you find it difficult to get rid of your negative biases.

There is another very common reason that hinders our gratitude processing. This hindrance can also be seen in people who have not been struggling in any way and have been largely happy in their lives. The hindrance to their gratitude can be their sense of entitlement to the lack of acknowledgment of their dependency. For instance, an angsty teenager can feel entitled to have the new PlayStation, and even when his parents buy the game for him, he might not feel appreciative because he never consciously even thought about him being dependent on his parents for such things. The best way to deal with this tendency is to actively promote someone else's business/good traits/ethics at least once a day. Doing this will make you look closely at what others are working hard on, and will also allow you to appreciate their efforts. This can prove to be a significant step in your gratitude journey.

Tools and Exercises

After recognizing and dealing with the hindrances that are blocking your gratitude, you can move forward and adopt some simple methods that can help you inculcate gratitude in your daily routine. Gratitude is the key to your happiness; therefore, you must adopt these practices in your daily routine to see a substantial change. You must do it even if it seems silly at first, or even if you feel that it would not help you much. Just read the methods one by one and embrace them for at least a week. Note that the more methods you adopt out of the following, the more difference you will see after a week. Let us get to the exercises straight away:

Keep a Gratitude Journal

This is the most common method to improve your gratitude game and it is also the most effective one. You can choose a time of the day to write in your journal the things you are grateful for. I would suggest you either do it first thing in the morning, or at the end of the day (just before you go to sleep). For the first couple of days, try to write anything that you are grateful for, anything that comes to your mind. For instance, you can write that you are thankful for your family, for your luxurious life, and so on. But then, we should move towards writing about things that we are genuinely thankful for and touched by. The magic is in the details. So, after writing one-word/one-sentence points for the first couple of days, try to write at least two to three sentences about each of the things you are grateful for on the third day. It does not matter if you are writing about ten things you are grateful for or just one thing. You just need to be able to genuinely feel its value in your life and your genuine thankfulness.

Writing Gratitude Letters

This was first suggested by Robert Emmons in his book Gratitude Works! (Johnson, 2020). Writing in your journal is something very personal and something just for you. However, to be more joyful we must radiate this joy and spread it. So, if you find yourself writing in your gratitude journal about someone helping you and/or loving you unconditionally, do not just express this gratitude in your journal. Write a thank you letter to this person and be vocal about your gratitude. It will make you feel satisfied, and make the other person happy and appreciated as well. However, if you feel too shy or uncomfortable with the idea of writing a letter, you can try expressing yourself in a long text message/Instagram DM, or a handwritten note on a Greeting Card. You can use your social media platforms sparingly for this purpose; even comments on pictures/posts can convey your gratitude. Doing this will simply allow you to share your goodwill and appreciation for the other person, which will surely make you feel very warm. It can also cement your relationship with the other person and create a new meaningful connection in your life. I know writing long text messages or letters can sound very cheesy at first, but once we get over the overthinking judgmental part of our brains, writing such lovely things to others can bring a lot of joy to our lives, and theirs as well.

Meditate/Pray With Gratitude

If you are religious or if you have a relationship with God or Universe, I would strongly suggest you pray daily and add gratitude to your prayers. You can ask God to help you in recognizing and vocalizing your gratitude, and you should also thank God for being with you this whole time. If you are not religious, I expect you have already added a meditation routine to your life. In that meditation routine, you can also add mindful contemplation about gratitude. You can thank yourself for being brave enough to fight your demons and to try to win over your depression, you can thank the universe for helping you through difficulties, and you can resolve during your meditation to be more grateful from now on. If you want to keep your prayers/meditation separate from your gratitude exercises, you can always add a special prayer/meditation routine to your day and ground yourself through gratitude. You can even add it to your nighttime routine and "count your blessings (instead of sheep)" before you sleep (Wikipedia, 2022).

Stop-Look-Go

This method is from David Steindl-Rast (Learning Lab Consulting, 2016) and it simply tries to slow you down. This is a method you can practice at any time of the day. The first step is to "Stop" doing whatever you are doing and take a break for a while, so that you can reflect. Then you must "Look" around and see what is in front of you, or hear what you can. Look into your own feelings at the moment and find out what you can feel grateful for at the moment. Then, ask yourself what work you need to do to make the world around you better and more loving. The moment you find an answer, "Go" and work on it. If you feel that preparing dinner tonight, or just spending time with family will bring more love into others' lives, and will portray your gratitude, then by all means do it. These little moments of reflection, analysis, and expression can be monumental in your life.

I have created this chart for you as an example so that you can include these exercises in your daily life. Following this chart would be ideal but you can always make some changes according to your preference.

Time of the Day	Gratefulness Exercises (Time Required)
Morning	Prayer/Meditation (5 minutes)
Noon	Stop.Look.Go (2 minutes)
Evening	Write a gratitude letter to someone/Write in you Gratitude Journal (5 minutes)
Before you sleep	Count your Blessings (1 minute)

So, following this chart would just take 13 minutes of your day, but if you keep following it consistently, these exercises will not even seem like exercise; they will become your lifestyle. Moreover, adopting these methods in your daily life will not only improve your happiness quotient but can also change how your brain is wired. When you treat gratitude as you treat brushing your teeth and eating, something called neuroplasticity occurs which transforms the structure and the working patterns of your brain. Therefore, you must follow these exercises to rewire your brain to be happy. Remember, this does not just apply to gratitude but all of the exercises in this book. However, if you find it difficult to come up with the things/people you feel grateful for, you can refer to this chart to make things simple.

What to Write in Your Gratitude Journal/Which Blessings to Count?
1. Start Simple: During harsh winters, you can thank the Lord for the warmth of the sun OR during summers, you can be grateful for the cool summer breeze.
2. List your Gifts: Ask yourself what you have in abundance and be grateful for it.
3. Who to Thank?: Ask yourself who made you laugh recently or who made you smile recently, and be grateful to them.
4. What's Necessary: Think about all the things you cannot live without. You must be grateful for them.

Take these methods as a grounding exercise that can help you be more aware and more conscious. We need to tune in to our surroundings and our relationships to extract the most out of them. But while extracting all the good parts, we need to share some of our goodness as well and gratitude is the best way to do it.

Gratefulness Comes Before Happiness

When going through a turbulent period in your life, it becomes difficult to actively practice gratitude. You might leave your exercises in the middle and feel like all your effort has been useless. Our mind keeps spiraling into the pit of negativity. Here, the only way to come out of the pit is to follow Nike's tagline: "Just do it." Snap out of it as soon as you can and get to work. To snap out of it, ask yourself questions like "What lesson can I be learning through this experience?" or "What part of my personality is being challenged here or is being improved upon here?". It takes practice to be better at anything. Even being our true selves requires practice and right now, you are changing your whole mindset and it cannot be done in one day. You have to be consistent, no matter what.

You might also ask—can we be grateful for everything? The simple answer is no. We cannot be grateful for violence/war/abuse/loss of a friend/unfaithfulness/exploitation. But we can always be grateful for the version of ourselves who has experienced such varied things and such pain, and still stands strong. Our end goal here is not just recognizing the moments/people we are grateful for, but living a grateful life by being completely aware of our present moment being a gift in itself. That is why life is given to us—to enjoy each moment and each gift it offers. Also, to be open to each and every opportunity to enjoy our gifts.

I have experienced that people who follow any religion, or any form of spiritualism are usually more open to opportunities and life's blessings. Robert Emmons (2007) perfectly describes why:

> As long as people have believed in God, they have sought ways to express gratitude and thanksgiving to their God, the ultimate giver. The great religious traditions teach that gratitude is a hallmark of spiritual maturity and a quality to be cultivated through spiritual disciplines. Gratitude is thus a universal religious sentiment, evident in the thank

> offerings described in ancient scriptures and in both traditional hymns and contemporary praise and worship choruses. (p. 91)

Therefore, it can be another task for a non-believer to open themselves up to such a huge change in perspective. But even if you do not believe, you can always be open enough to adopt a good habit. You can always observe how all religious people accept their life as a gift from God. You can accompany them to church/temple/mosque and just observe how their whole community works on gratitude and help. You can always learn more and adopt more goodness.

In this whole section I have deliberately asked you to force yourself to practice gratitude in life, whether you feel sad, or depressed, do not believe in the concept, or do not believe in God. Essentially, this was done to teach you that there is no prerequisite to gratitude. Happiness does not make us grateful, gratefulness is what makes us happy. "In positive psychology research, gratitude is strongly and consistently associated with greater happiness. Gratitude helps people feel more positive emotions, relish good experiences, improve their health, deal with adversity, and build strong relationships" (Harvard Health Publishing, 2011). So, keep working on improving your gratitude game to be happier.

Important Details to Remember

1. Gratitude is a deep emotional response to an act of goodness done to us.
2. Recognize the hindrances that keep us away from being grateful (like our negative bias, or sense of entitlement) and get rid of them.
3. Take a shortcut by turning the source of your negativity into the catalyst of your redemption.
4. Exercises for gratefulness: Keeping a gratitude journal, writing gratitude letters, meditating/Praying with gratitude, and stop-look-go technique.
5. Adopting these methods in your daily life will improve your happiness quotient and also change how your brain is wired through neuroplasticity.
6. You must live a grateful life by being completely aware of your present moment being a gift in itself.

7. There is no prerequisite to gratitude. Happiness does not make us grateful, gratefulness is what makes us happy.

CHAPTER 5: YOUR BELIEFS —FINDING THE MISSING POWER

Facts and speculations have always been around since humans could communicate well. Some things just are, while others can be. One way of knowing if something is a fact or fiction, is by seeing it with your own eyes or feeling it somehow through your other senses. However, there is a much more widely used, and much more productive method to know facts from speculation— simply asking why.

The higher power seems to be a faceless force like gravity. It is difficult to believe in it because you cannot see it, and do not even know if you feel it or not. But this lack of feeling/seeing does not guarantee that a higher power does not exist. We have to ask why. Just like we asked why we can stand on the earth without falling over if the earth rotates, which led us to gravity. So, ask yourself some "why" questions about your existence, purpose, and struggles to kick-start your journey.

For all the theistic people reading this chapter, I hope you will feel good about your faith by the end of it. Maybe this chapter will reignite your devoutness and give you solid reasons to continue believing in God, or a higher spirit. But all atheists and agnostic readers should know that I am not forcing you to be religious or spiritual or anything. Your devotion to God is solely your choice. I just want you to understand the significance of having a higher power in your life, especially if you are struggling.

Moreover, I believe if you can think about suicide, then you can also try anything that helps you feel better. No one else's God can help you ignite your faith or spiritualism. It is your own journey that you have to embark on. So, read this chapter with an open mind and try to analyze your own beliefs. There are no daily exercises in this chapter, just some simple changes that might be able to help you, and some questions that you should ponder over.

Who/What Is the Higher Power?

Higher power can be anything/anyone. For some people, it is God. For others, it is the Universe and its mystical laws. If you do not believe in any of those, you can still have your own philosophy/science behind how the world was created and what keeps it going, and believe in that.

All of the options mentioned above and your beliefs in them are valid. However, we still need to acknowledge that our civilization could not have flourished without religion. Religion, God and Jesus have been helping our civilization for ages, by bringing moral values and ethics to the table. Our ancestors, who have been following their religion for centuries, sacrificed their selfishness and helped their neighbors, they sacrificed their time and prayed to God, and put so much effort into building a trustworthy and dependable community. All these activities and sacrifices have added enormously to our current society's stability. Also, religion creates a conscience in people, which is way more powerful than any law the government can impose. Therefore, being religious has shaped our minds in such a way that we try to be as good as we can, not just for us, but for our society as well. This concept of goodness, in almost all religions, has been synonymous with the characteristics that can help a civilization flourish.

In different religions, God has been described differently. Some religions have multiple Gods and Goddesses, whereas some do not have a God at all. So, religion is a way of life that we can choose to follow, but our relationship with God goes deeper than that. Our faith in God brings out the best in us, encourages us to do better and strengthens us in tough times. We can place this faith in our souls as well. Theism is not the only way; we can be atheists and still practice and believe in, for instance, spiritualism. We can be non-religious but still believe in humanity as the higher power.

Essentially, the most important characteristic of religion and/or believing in a higher power (like God, universe, mother nature, energy, or soul) is a positive connection with the whole of humanity. This higher power gives us a set of beliefs that bind us to each other in a very metaphysical sense. Moreover, this connection brings forth the best that humanity can offer—love. That's why whenever we meditate or pray, it brings us a sense of being one with the world, and in love with all life forms, and this is what brings us peace because with connection and love, comes a sense of belongingness.

These feelings have other ways to take birth in you as well. Connect with people around you (positively), connect with nature, or connect with yourself. You can pursue any form of art (music, painting, cooking) to create this sense of love and connection. When you feel this loving connection to humanity and the world, you will have a sense of belongingness. And who knows, maybe on your way to feeling like you belong, you chance upon your version of God and find yourself talking to a higher power suddenly.

How to Believe?

I am no one to tell you how to find God. It should be your personal journey. Your meaning of a higher power would be the meaning that only makes sense to you. However, I will share some of the ways people turn into believers. There are two things you can do to seek this higher power—look outside yourself (read about different religions/philosophies) and look inside (introspect, meditate and find your driving force).

While looking outside is easier, to look inside and find a higher power, you need to be able to sit with yourself and think for longer periods. You can start with just spending five minutes with yourself each day and increase the time eventually. You must be observant of yourself and your own actions. You need to be patient for your inner journey to be fruitful. Meditate for longer periods and think about what your version of higher power could be. If during your meditation, you find yourself wishing for a better life or a soulmate, try to analyze who is on the receiving end of these requests. This can give you an idea of where your true belief lies. From there, you can build upon your relationship with this entity you consider every time you make a wish. Try to connect with them more often or try to talk to them. You do not need to pray specifically, just be yourself and talk to the entity. I am sure that after some time, you will have built a relationship with this entity, and talking to them will keep you centered.

In both of these inner and outer workings, you must practice patience. Faith is not something you can acquire overnight. It slowly plants roots in your mind and shoots up from there. If you feel you want to have faith and are open to trying anything, you must know that the first thing to do is to let your existing faith grow roots. But for your faith to grow into a strong tree, unmovable even during storms, you must nurture it every day. You must talk to your faith, and let it grow by letting go of your old, constricted patterns of thinking. After some time, you would have a good grasp of what your belief system is.

To get even deeper into our belief systems and adopt a faith, is it not more logical to ask why you should believe?

Why Have Faith?

When you try to meditate, and recognize the entity you had been praying to all this while and did not know, what do you feel? You will most probably feel supported. Especially when you are struggling, this support can be the difference between life and death. So your faith in a higher power will make you less lonely in your struggle and more resilient. A higher power is necessary because it acts like your trampoline—catapults you to heaven, or the best version of yourself, and protects you when you fall down. This supportive nature of religion has been the most beneficial for people who are struggling.

Moreover, scientific studies show theistic people to be more content in life, and more adept at handling problems (Sohn, 2010). This is because they not only gain a belief system, but a whole new community that believes in them. Congregations, chanting groups, religious services, and various religious events create an opportunity for all the believers to connect with other like-minded people, and increase their network. This religious community again helps us find a sense of belongingness in the world, and therefore, keeps us happy and satisfied.

There is another reason why religion has attracted so many of us throughout our history. Steven Reiss, a professor of psychology at Ohio State University says that there are 16 basic desires that we humans have: "acceptance, curiosity, eating, family, honor, idealism, independence, order, physical activity, power, romance, saving, social contact, status, tranquility and vengeance" (Ohio State News, 2015), and religion appeals to all of these desires. Therefore, it gives us a way of life that can bring us the most amount of fulfillment.

The most credible reason to have faith in a higher power is to give ourselves some hope. Hope for redemption, hope for a better life, hope for heaven, and hope for happiness. If you believe in a higher power, you will not be so anxious about what will happen in your life next, as you will trust your higher power to take care of you. This feeling alone can prove to be an important reason to believe in a higher power. However, your faith in God/Universe can even take you one step further than hope—it can take you to belief. Belief is not wishful thinking but presents a trust in the truth of our thoughts, however wishful they might seem. It is a massive leap from hope and can cement your relationship with God/higher power. But you should not have to force yourself to believe in anything. If you cannot accept it truthfully, it simply means that you cannot place your trust in it; if you cannot trust, you would not be able to receive joy in return.

Without a higher power that we can submit to, we would obviously believe that life took birth from nothing, has no meaning in particular, and has no purpose either (other than just surviving). This is a remarkably grim and sad perception of the world, and we have this perception only because we do not know precisely if there is a higher power out there. When we do not know anything, and when some vital questions have not been answered even by science, then why are we keeping only the most extreme options of explanation open for ourselves? Why are we choosing either to have complete faith, or to believe the grim reality of having no purpose? We must keep the other options open as well, instead of just belief and non-belief.

Agnostics are open to whatever the explanation can be, however, their stance is a very broad one, which does not have the capability to focus on a particular belief. This is not helpful either. So, what we need to do, if we consider ourselves atheists, is to open up a little and move towards the more logically correct stance of agnosticism. Then we must try to narrow down our flexible and varied beliefs into one or two explanations, so that we do not lack purpose or meaning. We would have to create our own new explanation of a higher power to direct our minds and utilize all that our life has to offer us. The idea is to be open to all concepts and beliefs that can help us lead better, fuller and happier lives. If religion can be one of those concepts, then so be it.

We humans have given birth to the most technologically advanced era. All this advancement was possible, only because we imagined something we could not see with our eyes, but only our imagination could clearly manifest. Our advancement is the result of thinking about what could be. A few examples of dreamers are the Wright brothers and Steve Jobs. Both inventors faced constant failures—Steve Jobs was fired from Apple and the Wright brothers had constant doubts from spectators, after their many unsuccessful flights. However, they never lost faith in their vision. Your faith can move mountains, you just need to fully surrender to it. Be patient and let your faith grow, as waiting is an important part of seeing the wonders faith can bring into our lives. It can answer all your prayers and fulfill all your wishes, as it did for Steve Jobs and the Wright Brothers. So, just try to be open enough to experience the love of a higher power and you might just be the next Steve Jobs.

You do not need to get rid of your rational and logical mind to believe. C.S Lewis, who received fame for his *Chronicles of Narnia*, was also famous for being the most reluctant convert from atheism to Christianity. He never got rid of his rationale, nor did he stop questioning the world after gaining his faith. I would like to share a similar story of a contemporary biologist/chemist and scientist, Dr. Sy Garte:

He was brought up in a militantly atheistic family, which went back three generations. So, obviously, he identified as a committed atheist, at first. However, as he grew up, he knew something was amiss. He, staying true to his parent's pride and his own beliefs at the time, went on to take up science as his career. He went deeper into biochemistry and found himself in the right place, as he was surrounded by other atheists. Almost all of the biologists he met did not believe in God. But for Dr. Garte, biology is what started his journey toward faith.

He was amazed at how peculiar the designs of life were. The spots on leopards, the patterns on a butterfly's wings, and so many different beautiful human beings on the earth were all coded with different and unique designs. Of course, other biologists noticed these designs too, but they assigned evolution to be the answer. However, for Dr. Garte, evolution was not the proper reason to be an atheist. He says that life cannot have evolved without the 99.99% accurate self-replication of living beings (via living cells/reproduction). After getting more into it, the question was, if evolution is not the reason for these designs, then what is? Is it a lucky accident? A gene from aliens? Or an intelligent designer of the world i.e. God? Other non-believing biologists have also asserted that evolution is not blind and has a purpose, as many studies suggest the same. So, there had to be a designer according to him. The more he read about biology, and even physics, the more he believed that the scientific explanations sounded like mysticism. So, he gave up his atheism and moved further to agnosticism.

On the other hand, while all this was happening in his work, his personal life was also moving towards flexibility. He was prompted by a friend to read the Gospels. He had read some of them in school just to reinforce his logical atheism. But this time around, he found credibility. He understood the resurrection of Jesus in the Gospels as plausible even though he noticed some contradictions. But these contradictions were similar to what any eye-witness account could have. While all this was happening, Dr. Garte had a very realistic dream, in which he was outside a walled garden. He tried to get inside the garden and went around the walls, but there was no way. He even tried to climb the wall but fell down. He was exasperated as nothing was working out when suddenly, a man appeared and asked him what was wrong. Dr. Garte told him about his predicament. The man smiled and said, "Why don't you use the door" and he pointed to the door right beside him in the wall. He had not seen the door earlier and so, asked the man what he needed to do to gain entry, to which the man replied, "Nothing, just open the door and go inside."

Dr. Garte was a scientist even when he had this dream, and knew that this dream might just have been a neurological/psychological phenomenon. Still, he knew he was getting closer to Jesus in every way. Somewhere, he knew that the man in his dream was Jesus, who was trying to help him get rid of the walls he had built around himself. Later, when he went to a church for the first time in his life, the first thing he saw was a picture of Jesus knocking on a door. He had never heard of "Jesus knocking on the door," and was yet to read about it, but he had somehow dreamt of it. At that moment, he knew in his heart that he fully believed in God and in Jesus as God's son. Now, Dr. Sy Garte is a devout Christian who feels that he was called to tell the world that science and God are not in conflict at all.

Dr. Garte's faith did not mature in a day, or even a week. It took years for him to truly understand the depth of God's love. So, if you open yourself up for a day, or a week, you might not see much difference. Honestly, there is no shortcut to faith. You have to trust in God and be patient. Rushing your faith would make things worse, as you would end up being closed once again because of not seeing results this early. You have to develop a true and honest belief, which will take some time to unlearn all the things you learned.

In the end, I feel that a higher power can help us as our parents did when we were young and still had a lot to learn. Just like our parents looked after us, even though we worked/played/studied independently, the higher power looks over us while we continue with our lives. This perception of faith gives someone more powerful, and more knowledgeable, the responsibility for our well-being. Even though the higher power does not interfere with your free will, you will experience some solace in the fact that someone trustworthy is always there for you even if you mess up sometimes. Moreover, almost all religions and faiths in the world aspire to give their followers some solid means to attain a peaceful and coherent mind. All their practices lead to peace and a sense of belonging, essentially. So, while you should stay away from bigotry, you must open your hearts to faith. If you feel a small little shift, then keep opening up; a new spirit is trying to come in, you just have to be inviting. Just a tip, when you are starting to open up more, you should start your bible journey with the book of James. It is only 5 chapters long and will tell you how to trust God and live a good life.

Important Details to Remember

1. Ask yourself some "why" questions about your existence, purpose, and struggles to kick-start your journey.
2. If you do not believe in God/Universe, you can still have your own philosophy/science behind how the world was created and what keeps it going, and believe in that.
3. The most important characteristic of believing in a higher power is its positive connection with the whole of humanity. You can connect with people around you (positively), connect with nature, or connect with yourself to experience this goodness.

4. There are two things you can do to seek this higher power—look outside yourself (read about different religions/philosophies) and look inside (introspect, meditate and find your driving force).
5. Why we should have faith: for emotional support, to never feel lonely, to have a good community with the same beliefs, to bring the most amount of fulfillment, to give ourselves hope, and because the alternative is too grim.
6. Almost all religions and faiths in the world aspire to give their followers some solid means to attain a peaceful and coherent mind. Isn't this exactly what we need?

CHAPTER 6: THE MANTRAS YOU NEED

Affirmations

You might have come across the term "affirmations" at some point in your life. These are concise and positive statements about ourselves. They help us be more positive and happier when we read them out to ourselves every day, and if we honestly believe what they convey (even better if you do it in front of a mirror). However, it can be hard to do because of our own inhibitions. We might think they are too corny! However, as we discussed in the previous chapter, the point is to try things that can help us, even if we have an adverse reaction to them at first. Actually, it would be better if it challenges some of the walls you have built around yourself because that would mean that these affirmations can knock those walls down, and let you be more vulnerable.

What exactly are we trying to do here? We are trying to convince ourselves to believe in the things we find difficult to believe about ourselves at the moment. Sometimes, when we feel lost or overburdened by life, it becomes difficult for us to keep a positive outlook. However, if we continue to repeat these affirmations about ourselves, we can force our minds to accept these as the truth.

To gain the most benefits, we must do it right. Firstly, we must find the precise reason why we need affirmations, only then can we make any progress. So, we must use the right affirmations for certain feelings/emotions (the ones we need to fight). Once we do this, we should visualize our affirmations clearly in our minds while saying them out loud. Also, we must try to feel the positive feelings associated with them. Only if we do all these things simultaneously, can we actually feel and believe the benefits.

However, you must remember that affirmations and mantras are like band-aids; they are pretty good when we need to cover the wounds and stop the infection, but they do not aid in healing. So, you can use these when you find it difficult to continue working on yourself because of sadness, depression, anger, or toxic people. These can help you stay on track to get rid of all your sufferings, but these cannot be the only means to heal you. I have created some lists of affirmations for you to repeat to yourself, according to the emotions you want to fight. You can choose the ones that resonate with you the most, or you can even customize them according to your needs. Repeat these time and again, whenever you require, for however long you need.

When You Are Feeling Depressed

- I am kind to myself and forgive myself for feeling inadequate or depressed.
- This too shall pass.
- I forgive myself for all my mistakes.
- I acknowledge my past trauma and choose to heal from it.
- My past has no power over me.
- I allow myself to heal in whichever way possible.
- I will heal at my own pace.
- I am patient with my progress.
- I will take one thing at a time/one day at a time.

When You Are Feeling Anxious/Angry/Sad/Frustrated

- I release all my tensions and fears.
- I let go of things I cannot control.
- My mind has the power to shape my life, and I have the power to shape my mind.
- I can do anything I set my mind to.
- All my emotions are valid.
- I am in charge of my emotions.
- I am the owner of my mind, body, and soul.
- Uplifted thoughts equal uplifted life.
- I choose to focus on my blessings. I choose positivity.
- I am responsible for my happiness.

When You Are Feeling Hopeless and/or Worthless

- I am proud of myself for being a fighter.
- I am enough.
- I am worthy of all the happiness and comfort in life.
- I welcome friendships and love with open arms.
- My existence in this world makes a difference. I make a difference.

- I am loved by my family, friends, and God.
- I am on the path God/the Universe deems best for me.
- I am a winner and I have endless possibilities for success.
- I am the writer of my story.
- Nothing and no one have the power to damage me for good.
- I will always have abundant opportunities before me.
- I am safe under the loving energy of God/the Universe.
- I am peaceful and content with myself. I deserve to be at peace.

When You Are not Feeling Good in Your Body

- My body is capable of regenerating, and I am capable of directing it.
- My imperfections are perfect as they make me unique.
- I am proud of my uniqueness.

- I am safe in my body.
- My body is wonderful as it allows me to enjoy my life and experience various things.

When You Feel Tired of Life

- I have the ability to create the life I want.
- I am inspired to be productive every day.
- I am living to my full potential.
- My life is a gift, and I am enjoying it fully.
- I am grateful for my life.
- I am living in the present and creating my future.

When You Are Being Patronized

- I surround myself with people who uplift me.
- I stay away from toxic personalities.
- I can always say "no" to things that do not serve me well.
- I trust myself to do the right thing.
- I feel empowered.

Meditative Chanting

Studies "suggest that chanting may be an effective tool for enhancing mood and creating a sense of social cohesion. These benefits, in turn, may be associated with increased health and wellbeing" (Perry et al, 2016). These chantings must be vocalized in a rhythm and multiple repetitions to gain the most benefits. The combination of your sound, rhythm, and breathing is what determines the efficacy of the mantra meditation. I have provided four different chanting mantras here, along with their meanings. You can choose anyone, or chant all four at various times of the day, or whenever you feel like connecting with your mind and body.

Chanting short mantras repeatedly is also called "*Japa*" in Sanskrit, which is typically done along with a string of "*rudraksha*" beads (or mala). This "mala" has 108 beads in total, and we can count the number of times we have chanted the mantra by passing the beads through our fingers, one by one. This is just an option though, not a necessity. What is necessary is your strong intention, will, and concentration. However, if you sense your thoughts deviating from the chant, or if you are distracted, do not worry. Distractions and wavering thoughts are normal, just recognize when this happens and slowly bring yourself back to the chant. Let's get into it then.

1. Om

In Hinduism, Buddhism, and Jainism, you will find that many mantras and prayers start with the Sanskrit word "Om". It symbolizes the supreme consciousness. In Hinduism, "Om" is the sound of life and our cosmic world.

While pronouncing "Om," you must carefully enunciate each syllable-"Aum." Remember that the "m" sound at the end should be prominent and pronounced for a longer time than the first syllable. You must take a long breath, then while exhaling slowly, utilize about ten seconds to pronounce "Om" once. Then you can take another breath and pronounce the complete word for 10 seconds, once more. A longer duration of pronouncing "Om" has been said to be a powerful catalyst for a deeply spiritual experience. You can also amplify the healing sound of the word by closing your ears with your thumbs and chanting for five minutes. Once you finish chanting "Om" for five minutes correctly, you will come out of the meditation feeling more centered and rejuvenated, for sure.

2. Tayata Om Bekandze Bekandze Maha Bekandze Radza Samudgate Soha

I know it is a mouthful, but it is abundant with meaning. This Buddhist mantra is called the Medicine Mantra and it is chanted to relieve pain, sickness, trauma, and even depression. It asks the higher power to carry us beyond this cosmic world, eliminate our sickness, our pain, and our suffering along with all the causes of our suffering, and lead us to the abundant ocean of goodness and purity.

This mantra is also believed to remove negative energy and frustration from our daily lives, as it asks for Nirvāna. At first, you can sit calmly with your eyes closed and play this mantra on YouTube to get a hint of its pronunciation. After some sessions, you might find it easier to pronounce and remember. Once comfortable, you can chant this medicine mantra for five to ten minutes every day.

3. Nam Myōhō Renge Kyō

This chanting mantra comes from Nichiren Buddhism and is a fairly easy one to pronounce. It is based on Nichiren Buddhism's belief in the Lotus Sutra and symbolizes devotion to the mystic law (of the Lotus Sutra) and a life of various possibilities. However, the meaning is much deeper than that. The word "*Renge*" denotes lotus blossom which blooms even when planted in muddy waters. It alludes to our strength which is only brought forth when we suffer in life. The word "*Kyo*" denotes the threads of the fabric of life, made up of both—fundamental existence as well as regular life. It signifies that our life is made up of both, our fundamental truth and our daily busy lives. If any thread is out of place, the whole weaving of the fabric of life will be marred. So, we must create a balance and keep on weaving.

So, "*Nam Myōhō Renge Kyō*" can be chanted to increase your life force and to establish a dignified regular life.

4. Asato ma Sadgamaya, Tamaso ma Jyotirgamaya, Mrityorma Amritam gamaya.

This is a prayer from *Brihadaranyaka* Upanishad and is quite deep. Its exact definition is: From illusion/falsehood (unreal), lead me to the truth (real); from darkness, lead me to light; from mortality, lead me to immortality. Chanting this prayer can help you be centered and focused in your life. It will remind you of your purpose in life and will give you direction to pursue it. If you find it difficult to pronounce right now, you can always hear it on YouTube first.

Chanting any of these, or even all of these regularly will surely leave an indelible imprint on your mind. The vocalized and repetitive chanting will work on your breathing patterns and energize you. Studies confirm that "repetitive speech induces a significant reduction in thought-related cognitive processes" (Berkovich-Ohana et al., 2015) which is what calms our minds and keeps us centered. You can even try to chant when you feel anxious or deeply sad, and it will calm you down. However, if you are not a fan of eastern chanting and meditation, read on.

Christian Meditation

If you have a relationship with the Lord Jesus, Son of God and believe in him faithfully, you can always ask him to guide you and to have mercy on you. You can do this as a meditation as well, that too, anywhere and at any time. You should take a deep breath in while saying "Lord Jesus," and breathe out while saying "Have mercy on me/Guide me." You can say these words out loud if you want to, or you can repeat them in your mind if you are outside (while walking, shopping, or eating).

Or you can meditate composedly in a peaceful environment, with 20 minutes spare in your schedule. In this meditation, the methodology has been borrowed from eastern meditation, but with Lord Jesus and the bible in mind as well. While meditating, you must remember what God has done for you, you must remember all the lovely things God has provided you with in this world and be thankful for the Lord's love. You can also go through these meditative thoughts while reading the word of God, or you could play any guided Christian meditation video on YouTube as well. I will give you an example of how you can do this.

Sit calmly and comfortably in a chair, bed, or wherever you feel like sitting. Take a long breath. Then, set an intention to not rush through this. Slow your thoughts down, and close your eyes. Notice the sounds around you (the sound of the fan/AC, the sound of distant traffic, or the chirp of the birds outside), then notice the sound of your thoughts (what tone you have, or what is troubling you). Focus on your body, starting from your feet, your ankles, your calves, and eventually the center of your forehead. Once you reach your forehead, you can start focusing on your breath—

count to four, slowly, while you breathe in; hold your breath for two seconds and breathe out while counting to eight.

Draw your attention and awareness to the presence of God. He has been with you all this time, and it is time you acknowledge his presence. Imagine Jesus placing his hands in yours showing his love and support for you. Once you feel his presence around you, you can start reading and then, repeating these bible verses. You can also learn a couple of verses from the following, if they resonate with you, and repeat them in your mind during this meditation. All these verses have been taken from the Common English Bible:

- It's impossible to please God without faith because the one who draws near to God must believe that he exists and that he rewards people who try to find him (Hebrews 11:6).
- Throw all your anxiety onto him, because he cares about you (1 Peter 5:7).
- In God, whose word I praise. I trust in God; I won't be afraid. What can mere flesh do to me? (Psalm 56:4).

- But the Lord is the one who is marching before you! He is the one who will be with you! He won't let you down. He won't abandon you. So don't be afraid or scared! (Deuteronomy 31:8).
- Let the Lord give strength to his people! Let the Lord bless his people with peace! (Psalm 29:11).
- Certainly the faithful love of the Lord hasn't ended; certainly God's compassion isn't through! They are renewed every morning. Great is your faithfulness (Lamentations 3:22-23).
- The Lord is good to those who hope in him, to the person who seeks him. It's good to wait in silence for the Lord's deliverance (Lamentations 3:25-26).
- I can endure all these things through the power of the one who gives me strength (Phillipians 4:13).
- I foresaw that the Lord was always with me; because he is at my right hand I won't be shaken. Therefore, my heart was glad, and my tongue rejoiced. Moreover, my body will live in hope, because you won't abandon me to the grave, nor permit your holy one to experience decay. You have shown me the paths of life; your presence will fill me with happiness (Acts 2:25-28).

- (A psalm of David) The Lord is my shepherd. I lack nothing. He lets me rest in grassy meadows; he leads me to restful waters; he keeps me alive. He guides me in proper paths for the sake of his good name. Even when I walk through the darkest valley, I fear no danger because you are with me. Your rod and your staff–they protect me. You set a table for me right in front of my enemies. You bathe my head in oil: my cup is so full it spills over! Yes, goodness and faithful love will pursue me all the days of my life, and I will live in the Lord's house as long as I live (Psalm 23:1-6).

- Don't be anxious about anything; rather, bring up all of your requests to God in your prayers and petitions, along with giving thanks. Then the peace of God that exceeds all understanding will keep your hearts and minds safe in Christ Jesus (Phillippians 4:6-7).

- I've commanded you to be brave and strong, haven't I? Don't be alarmed or terrified, because the Lord your God is with you wherever you go (Joshua 1:9).

- The mountains may shift, and the hills may be shaken, but my faithful love won't shift from you, and my covenant of peace won't be shaken, says the Lord, the one who pities you (Isaiah 54:10).
- Don't fear, because I am with you; don't be afraid, for I am your God. I will strengthen you, I will surely help you; I will hold you with my righteous strong hand (Isaiah 41:10).
- Every scripture is inspired by God and is useful for teaching, for showing mistakes, for correcting, and for training character, so that the person who belongs to God can be equipped to do everything that is good (2 Timothy 3:16-17).

However, if you feel that chanting mantras help you more, you can always chant the Christian mantras and feel the Lord's love. These will bring a breath of fresh air into your life and encourage you to hold your ground. These are some of the Christian mantras (that have been borrowed from the Common English Bible and edited to make them easier for you to chant):

- If you confess with your mouth "Jesus is Lord" and in your heart, you have faith that God raised him from the dead, you will be saved (Romans 10:9).
- Do not grieve, for the joy of the Lord is your strength (Nehemiah 8:10).
- I can do all things through Christ who strengthens me (Phillippians 4:13).
- Those who seek the Lord, lack no good thing (Psalm 34:10).
- I will not stumble for the Lord is right beside me (Psalm 16:8).
- Happy are those who are humble; they will receive what God has promised (Matthew 5:5).

When you choose to recite affirmations, meditate, or chant, you are automatically treading towards spirituality, which lays a solid foundation for your mental health. Moreover, by doing this, you are stepping into your strengths and altering something in your soul. If you experience peace after meditation and/or chanting, you are clearly doing something right for yourself. At this crucial stage of your life, when you are facing such difficulties, this little act of caring for yourself can work wonders. You should do these kinds of activities more and care for yourself.

Important Details to Remember

1. Through affirmations, we are trying to convince ourselves to believe in the things we find difficult to believe about ourselves at the moment.
2. Affirmations and mantras are like band-aids; they are pretty good when we need to cover the wounds and stop the infection, but they do not aid in healing. Don't take them as the only means to heal you.
3. Meditative chanting can play a huge role in your overall wellness, as it connects you to your mind and body. It will calm your mind and keep you centered.
4. If you have a relationship with the Lord Jesus, you can meditate in his name and by reading bible verses. You can also take help from guided Christian meditation-videos, or you could even chant bible verses as mantras.

CHAPTER 7: SELF-LOVE

You are altogether beautiful, my darling; there is no flaw in you. —Song of Songs, 4:7

We have been created in the image of God, who is ethical, just, and loving. We all have these capabilities within ourselves that allow us to move forward in our lives. Our personalities are all different and unique as we grow up in different environments, and with different belief systems. All this, along with the knowledge and experience we gain during our lives, is what constitutes our whole being. You have been following this book and have been on a journey to rediscover yourself. However, if you keep doubting yourself, patronizing yourself, and comparing yourself with others, you will never achieve your goal. You need to be able to accept and love yourself to move further in your journey to happiness.

This self-love is about feeling good in your own skin and personality; it is about being your true self, and increasing your own value in your eyes, even when you acknowledge all your faults. Self-love also includes self-care in its definition. So, loving yourself would mean that you care enough to do the right thing for yourself. If you love junk food, eating it is not self-love because you know it is not healthy for you. But if you try not to eat junk food much, and only eat it sometimes to treat yourself—this becomes a small act of self-love.

There are two main enemies of self-love–comparison with others, and negative self-talk. As we discussed in the previous chapters, comparing yourself with others is meaningless because nothing in life is perfect and no one's life is perfect either. On the other hand, we have also discussed how we can recognize our thoughts even before they become concepts to nip the negativity in the bud. I am sure you have been following these methods, and are ready to move forward confidently.

To move forward, we must focus on our strengths and appreciate them. When we know our strengths and focus on them, we will automatically like being ourselves. We would gain more trust in our capabilities and would be able to direct our lives in a better way. Always remember that you are responsible for your life, and therefore, you are also responsible for the love you receive. This is another reason why you should indulge in self-love, for if you do not love yourself, you will behave in a way that will lead others not to love you either because you would radiate the feeling of being undeserving of love. To prevent such unfortunate instances from happening to us in the future, let us see how we can love ourselves better.

How to Love Yourself

Just like avoiding junk food is a small act of self-love, there is so much more that you can do for your body that will always make you feel good about yourself. Some of the things you would already know, for instance, taking a shower every day, brushing your teeth twice every day, and so on. Hygiene is important, but do not forget your gut health, physical activity, and sleep routine. You should always eat freshly prepared, home-cooked meals that you cook yourself; you must move around throughout the day (while a gym is a good option, but your movement should not be just limited to the gym), and you should sleep for at least seven hours every night. This is the bare minimum that you can do for yourself. Some busy days or special occasions are fine to give yourself a cheat meal, or a rest day, but you must come back to your routine soon.

If you take care of your body as suggested above, you will see sure-shot changes in how your body looks. However, changing your body should not be your motivation. You need to learn to love your body regardless of its looks. Your body is a gift that allows you to see beautiful sunsets during your evening walks without getting too tired, and experience thrilling sports with agility. It allows you to do your work and live your life. So, it is only fair that you be grateful for your body and take care of it, in return. So, no matter how your body looks right now, just keep moving around, eating healthy, and taking care of it. Give your body some love.

You can also try to organize your living space and declutter your room/house. More organization and cleanliness equal more peace and calm. Moreover, organization and decluttering can even help you get a little motivated about your day. Even if you do not feel like getting up and doing anything, if you just force yourself to do some organizing around your space (making your bed, cleaning your work desk, organizing your wardrobe), you will instantly feel energized and ready to work some more.

If you are new at this, you should also add some self-love affirmations to your daily affirmations. Add and customize your already existing ones by including "I love my whole being." While saying your affirmations in front of the mirror, also say— "[your name], I love you" repeatedly. This will feel weird, at first. But I am sure, by now you know how doing the work is way more important than overthinking about it or judging it. You can also leave some beautiful notes for yourself in your purse, the book you are reading, or even your refrigerator. For instance, you can write: "Thank you for accepting me as I am and being kind when I struggle. We are on a wonderful journey together where we love, laugh, cry, and experience true faith; this would not have been possible without your open heart. I love you deeply for all that you are and for all that you are not." You will feel wonderful reading it later when you stumble upon it, especially if you are having a hard day.

There are so many other things that you can do for yourself. You can take long walks with your pet, meditate/pray, watch old films you loved as a child, read your old comics/books, prepare and enjoy a meal alone, watch the sunrise with your favorite beverage, note down some optimistic thoughts/wishful thinking, or remind yourself to smile for no reason. All these can count as little acts of self-love. Do whatever makes you happy and peaceful—pamper yourself. Keep some days on your calendar schedule for yourself and list down all the activities you would love to do on that day. DO NOT be lazy about this. You must show up for yourself, just as you show up for your kids/parents/spouse/close friends. Be your own best friend. You are equally important to yourself, if not more, and you should learn to count on yourself. Make a list of all the activities you would like to do and then tick them off the page when you're done with them.

You must also have some very positive and loyal friends so that you can receive love and support from others as well. Improving your social skills and maintaining a tight circle of good friends can do wonders for your self-love. They can bring you up whenever you are feeling down. They can motivate you whenever you feel lazy/frustrated. You would also be able to vent some of your anger by sharing your problems with them. Spend time with them and be there for them as well, if they need you. Maintaining good friendships (even with family members) can be like an investment that will always give you good returns. If you do not have such a circle of friends right now, you can always create new friendships. You can create accounts on apps like Meetup and meet new people who like the same activities as you do. You can also join Facebook groups where all the members can schedule when they can gather together and hang out. You just have to be willing to try, and new options and avenues of friendships will open up.

Another very fun idea for you to show some love to yourself is laughter. Laughter really is the best medicine. If you have a good friend circle and very close familial relationships, you can get together with them and have fun at the bar, or you can plan a comedy movie night with them. You could also plan to watch live games together. Just try to put yourself in scenarios where you hang out with loved ones and laugh together. If this does not work out, you can watch those movies/games/sitcoms alone as well, as you should be able to spend some time alone. You can also book tickets to a stand-up comedians show nearby. Just try to have fun so that you laugh heartily. Laughter can make you forget about your worries and can instantly put you in a better mood.

However, the most important act of self-love you can ever do is to set boundaries with people. If you do not want to go to your colleague's party, say "no" before it is too late, or before it becomes awkward for you. If you do not want to spend your "Self-love" day with your gym buddy, tell them the same. Tell your colleague how you cannot help them with their workload, as you pre-planned this free time by working extra hard earlier. However, setting boundaries is not about saying "no" all the time. It is about being honest about your time and preferences with others. When you value your time, others will start valuing it too. You just need to clearly and honestly express yourself.

In the end, while doing the work on loving yourself, do remember to celebrate all your small victories. If you had a wonderful day of self-love, and feel amazing about yourself, celebrate your effort by having your favorite dessert. If you worked hard on a project and finished it in time, celebrate this effort with a day of oversleeping a little. You can celebrate your small wins however you want and whenever you want. Celebrating them would keep you motivated as they will feed your pride and your self-worth, and it can also help you to not get tired after just two or three rounds of hard work.

How to Heal With Self-Love

What if we keep doing all the acts of self-love but do not understand their significance in life? We must keep reminding ourselves of the purpose of this journey, which is happiness and peace of mind. We need to heal ourselves to be our true selves, and to heal, we must practice self-love in a meaningful and more spiritual way.

Before you start this healing process, I want you to imagine your mind space as a safe and peaceful house. You are in charge of who can or cannot come into this house. You also have a white door in the house, which leads to an open backyard. So, if you let some doubts and lies about yourself inside by mistake, you still have the option to take them with you to the other side of the white door and leave them there. You must resolve to no longer let them in your house. But these doubts and lies will come knocking on the door and ringing the doorbell. They will always want to intrude. So, you must always be prepared to selectively let your emotions inside. For the happiness thief—toxicity, you must be locked and loaded with your pristine armor of self-love and self-respect.

You are your best friend and confidante. Your relationship with yourself is the most important one that you could ever be in. So, you must consciously try to change your perspectives while you indulge in your self-love routine. Eventually, you will be able to merge these perspectives with your other daily thoughts and viewpoints. The first change in perspective is about the difference between self-love and selfishness. Taking time out for yourself, or choosing yourself over useless activities that are not helping anybody, is not selfish but a part of your self-care routine. Self-care and self-love do not equal selfishness. Instead, they help you be a better and more loving person. You must keep filling yourself with love to share it with others. Think of it as a pyramid of empty glasses. You are the top glass, so only when you are overflowing with the wine of love will you be able to pour the extra wine into the other glasses.

When you start taking self-love days, try to do only the activities you truly enjoy. Do not be influenced by others but only trust yourself. One trick that can help you choose what you would enjoy more is living in the present, and for the present. See what mood you are in and how you are feeling physically, and then decide what can make you feel better. You will only enjoy the activity you are in the mood for and have the energy for. Also, try doing all these activities without any agenda/goal in mind. Just do them for the sake of fun. Live in the moment. However, along with living in the moment, choose to be consistent with your intention and activities. Do not miss your daily affirmations or reading your bible verses, as you cannot bring such immense changes overnight by not caring to be consistent.

Along with your relationship with yourself comes your relationship with God. Have a relationship with Jesus and get to know our creator. You can start with a simple hello! "Now faith is confidence in what we hope for and assurance about what we do not see" (Hebrews 11:1). You must believe that you will be picked up whenever you fall. And if, at any point, you find yourself crying for no apparent reason, well guess what my friend—you are in the presence of God. His soul is connecting with yours, and he is trying his best to get through to you. God created you in his image and does not want you to hate/hurt that image. You are full of love and light and he wants you to recognize it. We have a spiritual father who loves us unconditionally. But evil spirits keep trying to hold us back with doubts and lies. Whenever this happens, I want you to visually imagine these lies and doubts ringing your doorbell while you switch off the bell connection. Let them stand outside, and after some time, they will leave on their own.

Another change in perspective is to try and see the good in others as well, while you recognize your own goodness. Speak kind words to yourself and everyone, and take time to think before you speak. This will take a little practice at first, but eventually, you will get better. If you already see the good in people and are kind in your conversations, kudos to you! I know it can be hard to do these things when we are suffering ourselves. Words have immense power, so we should always try to say something good. Moreover, you must always act with love. You should radiate love. When you are kind and loving to not just yourself, but others as well, you will find deep satisfaction in being a good human being.

Important Details to Remember

1. Self-love is about feeling good in your own skin and personality; it is about being your true self, and increasing your own value in your eyes, even when you acknowledge all your faults.

2. There are two main enemies of self-love—comparison with others, and negative self-talk.
3. If you do not love yourself, you will behave in a way that will lead others not to love you either because you would radiate the feeling of being undeserving of love.
4. Things you can do for self-love: Organize your space, take care of your body, say self-love affirmations, leave loving notes for yourself, do what you enjoy the most, have a good loyal set of friends (or make some new friends), laugh a lot, and set boundaries with people.
5. While doing the work on loving yourself, you must celebrate all your small victories.
6. How to heal with self-love: by knowing that self-care and self-love do not equal selfishness; by recognizing that you are full of love and light, and God wants you to recognize it; and by trying to see the good in everyone.

CHAPTER 8: MEANINGFUL GOALS AND THE POWER OF GIVING

You have been working towards the right goal by reading and following this book's suggestions. This book has tried to create an urgency in you to experience the world quite differently and in a positive manner. This book has tried to open up another part of your life, and has reinvigorated the happy and full-of-life person that you were earlier. Moreover, after following all the mentioned steps, I trust that you have achieved some great objectives and goals. You should know how proud of you I am. You should be proud of yourself too.

During this journey, I believe you have felt a positive sense of achievement after every objective you finished. That is why you probably feel better than earlier. However, don't you want to experience this sense of achievement again and again? Don't you want to feel great about your efforts and your strength again and again? Of course, you do. So, even when you finish the book, you can keep achieving more and experiencing the satisfaction it offers. You can create your own personal goals.

Having and achieving personal goals have various benefits, most of which you might have already experienced. For instance, they give you a direction to focus your energy. So, even if you have been failing at doing something/achieving something, your effort will never go to waste because your concentration on achieving something will make you forget about your problems and keep you away from overthinking/anxiety.

Moreover, personal goals can also give our lives some meaning. With goals to achieve, we would never feel like a ship without a rudder. We will always have something meaningful to do. It will also give us a glimpse of the bigger picture, so we can have more clarity about where our lives are going. You must have experienced the rut of a repetitive daily schedule, like waking up, getting ready, going to the office/school, working, coming back, having dinner, sleeping, and repeating. This monotonous rut can turn into depression/anxiety very quickly. So, we need a few personal goals to keep us motivated and give us an incentive in terms of what we will receive after achieving the goal.

Also, setting personal goals will allow us to utilize our strengths and control our time. Both these activities can make us feel powerful. So, if I want to create a personal goal for myself, I would choose something I am interested in or feel I will be good at. This will automatically make me feel good about myself and will also prove to be a personal competition with myself. It will probably yield good results because I chose my goal according to my strengths. Compare these feelings with your feelings when you scroll Instagram/Facebook/TikTok endlessly. Which one do you think will make you feel better?

How to Approach Your Goals

Now we know what helped in this journey towards happiness and peace-setting and achieving personal goals. However, I want you to be adept at creating your own personal goals after you finish this book. I want you to use this book as a guide and create your own meaningful goals.

Firstly, let me clarify the whole concept of goals, objectives, and purposes. We sometimes use all these terms interchangeably, but they are very different. Please take a look at the following image—the concentric circles.

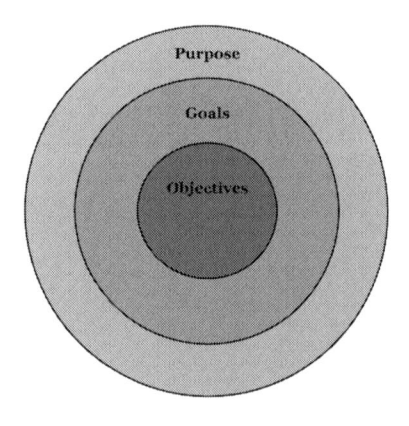

"Purpose" is the largest circle, "goals" is the second largest circle inside the purpose, and "objectives" have the smallest circle inside both the other circles. This image aims to clarify: Objectives<Goals<Purpose. Imagine yourself at the center of these circles. You will start finishing the objectives to reach the second circle of goals. The only way to reach your purpose circle would be by getting through the goals. We can have multiple objectives to attain our goals, and we can have three or four goals to reach our major purpose in life. These numbers of objectives, goals, and purposes are

not fixed. You can also have multiple purposes or more than four goals. The point is to have an idea of all three of these. Having all three will give you all the benefits we talked about in the previous section. Also, achieving these three by remembering the concentric circles will be vital for better results and satisfaction.

All of your goals and objectives should have a direction in life. They need to not let you be stagnant. Life keeps going on, and so should we. This is how we go on: First, focus on small objectives you can achieve to reach your goal. When you achieve your objectives, analyze the direction these objectives are taking you to—this should be your goal. For instance, you must focus on gratitude, forgiveness, faith, and controlling your emotions as your objectives to reach your goal of happiness. When you have achieved the goal, you must think about your purpose in life (a vision) to set the next goal.

Conversely, you could walk your mind back from the purpose you want to achieve in life. Then, you can work your way down to the goals and the objectives/steps you need to take to fulfill that purpose. Then, you can start with your objectives again.

Also, before you start working on your objectives to achieve your goals, you must think about all the obstacles you might face on your journey, and prepare for them in advance. This will not only prepare you for what is to come, but will also allow you to keep the complexity and achievability of your objectives/goals in check, so that you do not make your own life too difficult. There is another well-recognized way of achieving the goals that can help you—SMART goals.

SMART goal is a simple abbreviation for all the things you need to remember while setting your goals. Here, "S" stands for **s**pecific, "M" stands for **m**easurable, "A" stands for "**a**chievable", "R" stands for **r**elevant, and "T" stands for **t**ime-bound (MindTools, 2016). If we take care of all these factors when we set our personal goals, we would be good to go, as it takes all major nuances of goal setting into consideration. So, the next time you set a personal goal for yourself, keep all of these techniques in mind. You can even prepare a checklist for your goals and tick the SMART factors if they are present in your goal. For instance, if your goal is to learn to play an instrument, you must specify which instrument (fulfilling the "S" criteria of the SMART goals). Then you should see if you can measure your improvement from time to time. You should also see if your daily objectives to learn this instrument are achievable in a day or not. Then, ask yourself if learning this instrument is important to you, or others—find out its relevance. At last, give yourself a deadline to be on your toes and to be seriously committed to it.

You must also remember to keep a clear vision of your purpose in life while achieving all your goals/objectives. So, that you do not deviate and end up feeling like you wasted efforts on something unproductive. For this, you need to know what is important for you and what holds emotional significance in your life.

Which Goals Can Be Meaningful for You?

After learning about goal setting and achieving techniques, you must also know what kind of goals are considered meaningful enough for you to actually revel in their completion. Your personal goals are purely subjective. You must also know that while being an entrepreneur can be someone's purpose in life, you might not identify with it. You cannot look to someone else to give you a purpose/goal in life. You have to find something that is appealing to you.

How can you find goals that can be productive and meaningful for you? There are various types of goals and meanings behind them. The following can give you an idea of the direction you need to tread in. You can choose whichever idea excites you the most.

1. Goals that appeal to you emotionally: These types of goals can come from a conviction of yours. When you feel that your purpose can only be accomplished when you achieve a few smaller goals, these would be goals that appeal to you emotionally. These goals exist for a greater purpose. For instance, you could create a supportive community of helpful and compassionate friends or family to leave a legacy behind after your death.

2. Goals that let you be the best version of yourself/authentic self: These goals bring out the best in you and keep you happy. These goals will give you an improved living style and an improved sense of peace and happiness. They might be a little hedonistic, which is perfectly alright, as your purpose here would be to appreciate life as you only

live once. Doing what you enjoy the most and what seems to be the most exciting thing to do in life, would fall under these types of goals. For instance, traveling to gain more cultured experience, turning your passion into your career, or pursuing education just for knowledge's sake, would help you be your authentic self.

3. A calling/divine purpose of life: These types of goals/purposes can be both emotionally appealing and enjoyable as you feel you were born to do that work. Maybe you feel that God sent you into this world to achieve this purpose. For this purpose, you can work tirelessly to achieve any goal/objective. For instance, helping the needy, or doing God's work can come under these types of goals/purposes.

You might not know what exactly you want from your life right now, but you will find your purpose/calling soon. When you do, your life will automatically become more interesting and exciting for you. You will be motivated to do the work and celebrate the results. It is perfectly alright if you do not identify with any of the goal types I have listed above. Naturally, you would take time to find this sense of purpose again. But you can always look back to the childhood version of yourself; what did you want from life then? Remember your childhood dream, and start from there. Eventually, you will find your purpose/goal that inspires you, motivates you, and satisfies you.

Share Your Love and Kindness

Your purpose in life is going to be very subjective, of course. But because you want to feel happy and peaceful in the end, I would like to suggest a goal that you can include in your list of goals to achieve. I am sure it will make you feel very satisfied with yourself and your life. "Volunteering your time, money, or energy to help others doesn't just make the world better—it also makes you better. Studies indicate that the very act of giving back to the community boosts your happiness, health, and sense of well-being" (UCL, 2020). So, why shouldn't we try something that helps everybody?

Helping others can be started on a very small scale. We have already talked about gratitude and forgiveness previously, and how they can help us as well as others in feeling better.

There are other kinds of things as well, that are just little acts of compassion but can have a huge impact. So, if you are new to this, just try to smile more at people and ask them if you can help them in any way (not necessarily strangers, but your own family and friends). When you do not know how to help someone, the best course of action is to ask them directly but politely, preferably with a smile. You should be kind to others, especially when they require help. You will soon realize that doing this helps you feel good in your soul.

If you want to move ahead and help on a slightly greater scale, you can start taking care of animals as well. So many animals are stranded, mistreated, or even killed in the world. You can join organizations that help these animals and even adopt such an animal yourself. If you find it difficult to join such an organization, you can always help of your own volition. You can go out and feed the hungry and emaciated dogs/cats on the street, or build a small birdhouse and place it on your balcony/backyard, or keep some water for the birds on hot summer days.

You can also start donating things you do not use; like old clothes. However, do remember to clean them and sew any holes in them before you donate; we must be respectful even in charity. This is an easy practice that can make you feel good, because it cleared your clutter and helped someone in need. "A 2008 study by Harvard Business School professor Michael Norton and colleagues found that giving money to someone else lifted participants' happiness more than spending it on themselves" (Suttie & Marsh, 2010). So, you can also find some restaurants/cafés that provide the option of paying for someone else's (beggars/homeless people's) food. They take money from you and provide the food/beverage to the people who cannot afford to pay. This is also a simple and nice way to start helping others.

These acts of helpfulness allow us to be conscious of our choices and perspectives in life. When we start helping others, we start seeking and radiating goodness. When you start feeling the benefits of giving, you can go even further and teach someone for free. Don't worry! You do not need to take proper classes and lectures. You just need to help someone learn something new. For instance, you can teach your parents/grandparents how to use the new technologies in their phones/TVs, or you could teach your colleague some tips on something he/she had wanted to learn for a very long time. If you can, it would be great if you teach children at an orphanage.

You can also help someone in need through social media; you can post about the problems being faced and share it as much as you can. This is a great option as you would be able to track the improvement and the difference that your time and effort made as well. The likes and shares would help you have a wider reach and therefore, provide better help. It will let you clearly see what helpfulness can do and how powerful it can be.

However, nothing would be better than helping someone deal with depression and suicidal thoughts. Because of your own experience, it will be easier for you to understand their plight and help them with conviction. Moreover, if you successfully turn around their life, your own struggle would gain a purpose. The only problem here is that it is difficult to find people who are feeling suicidal as this is something nobody openly shares. So, the only way is to persuade them to open up. Pry out this information from your friends and family by writing this note to them:

"Unfortunately, suicide is on the rise and I want to put myself out there and give support to anyone who might need it. No questions asked, no judgment. If you just want to vent, I'm here for you. Feel free to reach me at 555-555-5555 or 123abc@gmail.com, or just inbox me. Whatever your method of communication is, I'm here for you! —Stay Blessed and alive."

This will at least give them the option to reach out. If you are comfortable, you can also add how you struggled with depression yourself and how you understand its grip on a person. Helping another person in need, especially someone you can relate to, will open you up even more. If you are there for people in the same position as you once were, it will heal even those parts of you that you couldn't heal. Share your experience with them and tell them what helped you. Give them this book if you think it might help, or if you don't have the right words to handle their despair. However, this good can only take birth once you spread the love and send a message to anyone who might be depressed and needs to talk to someone.

This act of kindness and compassion would make this world a little better. Our world is divided, not just politically but even mentally and physically. We have been separated from each other because of the cubicles in our offices, televisions/phones which have given us the luxury to stay in our homes, and movie theaters which have stopped us from talking to each other (even when we are all sitting together), and recently because of COVID-19 and the lockdown. However, helpfulness can counter this separation. Your acts of kindness and helpfulness can help you gain new relationships, based on trust and goodwill. It can create new meaningful connections.

Your kindness and help can actually never go to waste. Your helpfulness can help someone immensely, or it can at least improve their day and make them happy. Maybe your help clicked something in them and they got over the idea of committing suicide. Also, kindness always multiplies as your kind words can induce a good mood in both you and the other person. Then the other person might be a little kinder than usual and bring a smile to someone else's face, and so, can multiply the goodness.

Even when you donate food/clothes/money/blood/time, do not just donate and forget about it. To experience satisfaction, you should be able to see the difference your donation made. Choose the institutions that let you track how your contribution made a difference. When you connect with the community/individuals whom you are helping, you automatically feel happy about yourself. This can be the perfect goal for you to achieve right now, as it can help you fight your struggle too. Try helping someone today itself. If it makes you even a little bit happier, imagine how happy you would be when you do it regularly. By being helpful, you will leave a profound impact on this world and its people. Isn't that glorious!

Important Details to Remember

1. Having personal goals can give our lives some meaning and direction. They allow us to utilize our strength and time at the optimum level.
2. Objectives<Goals<Purpose. We must start finishing our objectives first, then move to our goals, and then to the purpose we wanted to accomplish.
3. All of your goals and objectives should have a direction in life, i.e., your purpose.
4. SMART Goals technique can help you set and accomplish your goals.
5. Meaningful goals for you: Goals that appeal to you

emotionally, goals that let you be the best version of yourself/authentic self, or a calling/divine purpose in life.

6. Acts of helpfulness allow us to be conscious of our choices and perspectives in life.
7. Your kindness and help can actually never go to waste.
8. Connect with the community/individuals whom you are helping to automatically feel happy about yourself.

CHAPTER 9: REAL-LIFE STORIES TO INSPIRE YOU

Carter Gaskins' Struggle

Carter Gaskins lived in West Virginia and had a difficult life since his childhood. He was bullied at school—he was called names, ostracized, and even punched and pushed at times. He wanted to share this with his parents. Still, he could not, as his father was a strong and silent man who never really appreciated showing true emotions. So, he used to cry alone and think why he couldn't be accepted by his schoolmates.

As he grew up, he started believing that he had to stick up for himself. This led him to hang out with the wrong people on the streets. These people with guns and gangs became his protection. He got into all bad things and realized how he still was not happy. However, his strong father's illness made him acknowledge this looming sadness. His father was the strongest man he knew, and he too was suffering and looking weaker by the day. His father's condition deteriorated, and he was put on dialysis. Looking at his helpless father, Carter started crying and shaking uncontrollably. This was when he had his first panic attack.

His father passed away three months later. He recovered and found the love of his life, Shanice. After another year, they were expecting a child together. However, the baby died shortly after the birth. That's when Carter felt the darkest. He felt overpowered by this huge dark cloud that surrounded him constantly. Things became so bad that there were multiple incidents when he held a gun to his head while sitting alone in his car, ready to end all the pain. His depression led him to separate from Shanice as well. She left him and went to Lawrence. However, Carter could not accept this loss. He followed her to Lawrence, and now says that it was Shanice who brought him out of the hellhole. He used this move as a new chapter in his life, and he learned to love and accept his life's beauty. This one decision of moving to Lawrence with Shanice saved his life by giving him a reason to continue on this colorful journey.

Now, he is a photographer with a purpose. He says he loves taking pictures of people to show them, no matter how they feel inside, that he and his lens can always see their beauty. He dealt with the pain and the frustration with the help of his wife and faced his demons head-on, which brought him out of his misery.

Kjersta's Story of Hope

Kjersta was in college when the pandemic hit. She had to leave her campus and her friends behind. It was difficult, but she knew she would get over it. Because of the lockdown, it wasn't just her friends that she could not meet, she could not go out anywhere either. Again, she thought that she would get over it. But in her loneliness, after some time, she found herself thinking more and more about things she had never thought about earlier. She was always brooding over the littlest of things. What else could she do? She was alone and could not go out. Her thoughts took a turn toward the negative pretty soon. She was now contemplating existential questions but in a very negative way. "What is the point of life?" she thought. She knew this question did not have an answer, but she could not stop her mind from answering it in the most negative possible way. That summer was when her depression started.

She felt suffocated in her room and even in her body. It became difficult for her to breathe sometimes during her panic attacks. However, her mind did not stop thinking. It started another conversation about how she was weak, and could not even handle staying alone. She felt helpless, lonely, and tired. Soon, she did not want to do even the basic daily chores. She just could not get up from her bed. There was no semblance of energy in her body. Her mind had now stopped thinking because it was sure about the answer to the question: There is no point in living, especially when you are this weak and useless. Kjersta felt numb. Even when her mother hugged her, and when her friends called her, she knew she wasn't the same.

After six more months, the suicidal thoughts started. She tried to find out the reasons people wanted to stay alive, but none of them were good enough for her. Moreover, during all this, she felt that maybe she was faking it; maybe she was so weak that she was calling her mood swings depression. She felt that other people had it worse and were in much more pain, especially because of COVID-19, and here she was acting like a crybaby for no reason. But she knew she had to reach out to someone when her menstrual cycle got messed up because of the depression. She felt so ashamed about her thoughts and feelings that she could not speak about them to the doctor. She wrote them down on paper and just handed them to her.

But reaching out proved to be the best decision for her. Her improvement wasn't linear at all. She was hospitalized five times and attempted suicide once, all while her treatment was going on. At times, she felt better, and at other times she was going backward. But she kept improving, felt better most of the time, and realized a few things about her treatment: She understood that hospitalizations were not to treat her during this time, but only to keep her safe. She realized how overthinking can take you to dark places and should be avoided. She found out that keeping a "crisis kit" nearby at all times helped her a lot, as whenever she felt there was no reason to live, she opened the box and found the things she had put in it when she was feeling better. It reminded her of the good things, experiences, and relationships she wanted from life. In the end, she realized that no matter how useless one feels, or how sad one is, you will get better if you just reach out.

Dess Butler's Experience With the Spirit of Suicide

When I was young, my father was the most loving and open father I could ever have hoped for. He was honest about all the things I asked, one of which was about his mother's (my grandmother's) suicide. He told me everything about it—how sometimes people cannot endure the pain life forces upon them, and they choose to end their lives. He also told me how awful his mother's death had been for everyone in the family. He was devastated and he still misses her sometimes. However, somehow my brain only retained that if life gets too hard, I had the option of committing suicide.

My family has always believed in Jesus, and I have always been a devout Christian, so I had faith to fall back on whenever the times were hard. I had quite a few hardships: My personal life, ministry life, and career had all taken a huge toll on me, I felt the spirit of suicide near me at times, but I fought it in the name of Jesus. However, there came a time when I had absolutely no idea how I would recover from the hardships. I found myself without a place to live, with three children to take care of. I was scared and had no idea how I would provide for my children. I still remember how I could not stop crying and started to pray. But this was the start of my mind taking me back to the awful and insidious spirit of suicide which was trying to creep back in. After a few days of struggle, I left my children with my sister and was driving back to do something about my situation. While driving back, I could feel the spirit of suicide entering my mind, and it put the thought of crashing the car and dying in my mind. I wanted to hit a big tree with full force, without my seatbelt on. I had encountered the spirit of suicide earlier as well, but it had never been able to convince the Christian in me. However, this time was different, and I felt that awful spirit's weight all over me. I remember taking a deep breath and hitting the accelerator. I was going to do it. My car was speeding up and I was determined. But suddenly, I saw three children on the side of the road. I was fast, so I passed them quickly, but I wanted to stop for them. They looked like my children. Just then, I heard the Lord's voice asking me if I care for those little souls. He made me hear my children's voices saying, "When will Mommy come back? Is she going to leave us here at the roadside?" I instinctively slowed the car down while bawling. I heard his voice again, "Have faith, I will help you." I stopped the car and started praying while sobbing. My prayers helped me lift the spirit of suicide from my body. I could still feel the brain fog it left, but it was much better than the suffocation of being trapped by its weight.

Fast forward a couple of years, I was better financially and mentally as well. However, I still sometimes felt the remnants of the spirit of suicide. While I was sitting in my room one day, I felt that awful spirit entering the room. I just could not understand why this spirit was not leaving me, even when I was happier. Then, I suddenly realized that I have never handed my life over to Jesus. I had put my faith in him but never completely surrendered. This is what the spirit of suicide was latching on to. So, I sat to pray and with all my heart gave the reins of my life to Jesus. I accepted whatever he had in store for me, I accepted however many days he had planned for me to live, and I gave Jesus permission to end my life whenever he deemed fit. I had already handed over my life to Jesus, but now, I handed over the end of my life to Jesus too. This is when the spirit of suicide completely vanished from my life. Now, I still feel sad sometimes and even frustrated, but I am still content with my life because I know Jesus will take care of me, no matter what.

Celebrities Who Survived Suicide

Owen Wilson

Despite having a great career, 2007 was a dark year for our beloved actor, Owen Wilson. Unfortunately, he got into drugs while suffering from depression. His drug problem escalated so much that Kate Hudson, his then-girlfriend, ended up walking out on the relationship. It is said that when Owen Wilson saw Kate Hudson with a new love interest, the pain tipped him over the edge. He overdosed and even slit his wrists. He was found by his brother Luke Wilson and rushed to the hospital. He was detoxed of the drugs and operated on his wrists by the doctors, saving his life. However, his brother Andrew helped him heal from the inside. He helped Owen by keeping up with his schedule so that the days seemed more manageable. His recovery was even more difficult as he is a celebrity, and the media was talking so much about this new interesting incident. The media, of course, talked mainly about his darkest moments. This would have been very difficult for him. However, with his brother's help and determination, Owen Wilson still continues to entertain us.

Drew Barrymore

Drew had a tumultuous past and an unusual childhood. Her parents divorced when she was nine years old. She was already a celebrity by then, and that completely overtook her childhood. At 13 years old, Drew was put in an institution when she came home drunk and started throwing things in her house. She even attempted suicide as she felt utterly lonely. She was just a child but was already a drug and alcohol addict at such a young age. It was all because of a lack of guidance from her parents and her celebrity status. Her condition made the judiciary decide that she could be emancipated at age 15. So, she moved out and started living on her own. She had to learn everything herself. She worked as a waitress and she even cleaned toilets, but no matter how dark her life got, she always remembered that there was goodness in life too. Now, with her vision and grit, she has achieved exactly what she wanted from life—a safe family space.

Key Takeaways

1. Work on your problems. Just like Carter moved to Lawrence, you can make huge changes (for the better) in your life too.
2. Stay away from overthinking, and always try to reach out. Help is always available.
3. Your faith gives you a lot of mental strength. Believe in something and rediscover your grit.
4. Family and friends must always be cherished, as they can bring you out of any mess you are in.

CONCLUSION

Your pain might be unbearable sometimes, and other times it might be non-existent. Sometimes, you feel elated with your life, while other times you might be frustrated. Life is nothing but a balancing act between the two extremes, so that we stay in the Golden Mean territory. Drew Barrymore did it, Owen Wilson did it, Carter and Kjersta did it too, and so can you. If you work hard on improving yourself and your life; if you are in control of your emotions, know when to give a f*ck, when to be kind, grateful, strong in your faith, helpful, and when to indulge in self-care from time to time, you will be the most satisfied and happiest person you have ever been.

I believe, no matter what you have done, or what has happened in the past, you will someday believe in the verses and affirmations mentioned in this book and stand strong. You must ingrain them deep in your soul. I did a lot of research for you and I was desperately trying to find answers to get to the other side without bringing up the existence of God or a higher power. However, there is not enough evidence to support this. But if you commit to making your life better and are not happy with how things are going right now, there is no reason why you shouldn't give God a chance. If you truly don't feel any positive emotion or shift in your mindset, that's okay too. At least then, you can't say that you didn't try.

What you are fighting for is something you can't see—your emotions, but you can feel them. We're not fighting against flesh and blood but against the spiritual forces that are unseen through our eyes, like anger, sadness, emptiness, frustration, helplessness, fear, guilt, depression, overwhelmed failure, sadness, jealousy, or thinking you are not enough. You have to consciously be aware of each emotion you feel, and how you react to those. There is a shortcut trick I would like to leave you with. You can refer to the following table to set an aim for your mind and transform all your negative emotions into positive ones.

Original (Negative) Emotions	Target Emotions/Concepts
Frustration	Gratification
Anger	Patience
Emptiness	Faith
Helplessness	Competence
Sadness	Appreciative
Loneliness	Independent
Failure	Learnings
Overwhelmed	Discipline/Control
Fear	Positive Imagination
Depression	Purposeful Existence

Target emotions/concepts are what you should focus on when you feel the emotions mentioned on the left side of the table. These emotions are not necessarily opposites but counterpoint each other well, and help you feel better. You should follow the tips this book provided in the earlier chapters and try to reach the "target emotions" whenever you feel the respective "original emotions." You will never really stop being sad/frustrated/angry because you are human and bound to feel those emotions from time to time. But now, you know how not to dwell on these emotions, and how to flip your switch and be in control. In the end, whenever you feel uncontrollable emotions, stop thinking about the original one and focus on the respective target emotion and how to achieve it.

Staying in a negative emotion will serve you no purpose. So, why choose to let it stay? Ask yourself questions about your feelings and moods. Try to figure yourself out, get to know yourself, and go deep to figure out the answers. You have it in you to change your situation and your life. I trust that you will soon be happier and more satisfied as you have already taken the first step. You will do it because it's your desire, intrinsic nature, and character. You are always willing to go to the other side where the light is, you just need to take the first step. Once you have, nothing can stop you from being happy. Cheers to your life ahead! Cheers to the new you!

REFERENCES

A quote by Sathya Sai Baba. (n.d.). www.goodreads.com. https://www.goodreads.com/quotes/7456167-before-you-speak-ask-yourself-is-it-kind-is-it

Berkovich-Ohana, A., Wilf, M., Kahana, R., Arieli, A., & Malach, R. (2015). Repetitive speech elicits widespread deactivation in the human cortex: the "Mantra" effect?. *Brain and Behavior*, 5(7). https://doi.org/10.1002/brb3.346

Betts, J. L. (n.d.). *30 Suicide quotes to encourage understanding & awareness.* LoveToKnow. https://dying.lovetoknow.com/words-comfort-after-death/30-suicide-quotes-encourage-understanding-awareness

Bible Gateway. (2011). www.biblegateway.com. https://www.biblegateway.com/passage/?search=hebrews+11%3A6&version=CEB

Borchard, T. (2015, August 4). *The second agreement: Don't take anything personally.* The Four Agreements. https://www.thefouragreements.com/the-second-agreement-dont-take-anything-personally/

Botes, J. J. (2017, November 5). *"Why Me?" a beautiful message by Arthur Ashe.* JAY BOTES. https://jayjbotes.com/why-me-a-beautiful-message-by-arthur-ashe/

Burkhead, J. (2020, August 28). Suicide prevention awareness: Stories of hope and resiliency. *LMH Health.* www.lmh.org. https://www.lmh.org/news/2020-news/suicide-prevention-awareness-stories-of-hope-and-resiliency/

Burns, T. (2009). Blessing those that curse you: On Lonergan, forgiveness, and the problem of evil. In S. Bloch-Schulman & D. White (Eds.), *Forgiveness: Probing the boundaries* (pp. 101–109). Inter-Disciplinary Press.

Emmons, R. (2007). *Thanks! How the new science of gratitude can make you happier* (p. 91). Houghton Mifflin Company.

Forgiveness. (n.d.). TheHopeLine.com. https://www.thehopeline.com/topics/forgiveness/

Garte, S. (2019). *Why I believe in the resurrection.* Peaceful Science. https://peacefulscience.org/articles/sy-garte-resurrection/

Harvard Health Publishing. (2011, November). *Giving thanks can make you happier.* Harvard Health. https://www.health.harvard.edu/healthbeat/giving-thanks-can-make-you-happier#:~:text=In%20positive%20psychology%20research%2C%20gratitude

Hattenstone, S. (2017, December 1). *Drew Barrymore: "My mother locked me up in an institution at 13. Boo hoo! I needed it."* The Guardian. https://www.theguardian.com/culture/2015/oct/25/drew-barrymore-mother-locked-up-in-institution-interview

Ibrahim, S., & New York Post. (2021, August 19). *Owen Wilson reveals his brother helped him after suicide attempt.* News.com.au.

https://www.news.com.au/entertainment/celebrity-life/owen-wilson-reveals-his-brother-helped-him-after-suicide-attempt/news-story/7f150a8d0e208879bb6de1cd3a2532a3

Johnson, B. (2020, September 14). *PNTV: Gratitude works! by Robert Emmons, Ph.D* [Video]. Youtube. https://www.youtube.com/watch?v=rC8uZwXN0dM

King James Bible. (2017). King James Bible Online. https://www.kingjamesbibleonline.org/ (Original Work Published 1769)

Learning Lab Consulting. (2016, October 31). *Stop, look, go: A mindful gratitude practice from David Steindl-Rast.* Learning Lab Consulting. https://learninglabconsulting.com/2016/10/31/stop-look-go-a-mindful-gratitude-practice-from-david-steidl-rast/

Lonergan, B. (2003). *Method in theology* (2nd ed., p. 117). University of Toronto Press.

Manson, M. (2021, August 12). *Everything Is f*cked: A book about hope - summarized by the author* [Video]. Youtube. https://www.youtube.com/watch?v=fEk5dhbNU70

Mihalache, G. (2009). Transformative Forgiveness: From Self-healing to Others-healing. In S. B. Schulman & D. White (Eds.), *Forgiveness: Probing the boundaries* (pp. 121–130). Inter-Disciplinary Press.

Mind Body Soul. (2021, April 9). *Affirmations for positive thinking, release negative thoughts, positive affirmations, manifest* [Video]. Youtube. https://www.youtube.com/watch?v=9A20iBiDcw0

MindTools. (2016). *SMART goals – how to make your goals achievable.* Mindtools; Emerald Works. https://www.mindtools.com/pages/article/smart-goals.htm

Ohio State News. (2015, October 5). The psychology behind religious belief. *The Ohio State University.* https://news.osu.edu/the-psychology-behind-religious-belief/#:~:text=Some%20have%20said%20people%20seek

Perry, G., Polito, V., & Thompson, W. F. (2016, July 5). *Chanting meditation improves mood and social cohesion*. ResearchGate. https://www.researchgate.net/publication/319851087_Chanting_Meditation_Improves_Mood_and_Social_Cohesion

SAVE. (n.d.). *Suicide survivor stories*. SAVE. https://save.org/what-we-do/grief-support/stories-of-hope/

Sohn, E. (2010, December 7). Why are religious people happier? *NBC News*. https://www.nbcnews.com/id/wbna40549161

Suttie, J., & Marsh, J. (2010, December 13). *5 Ways giving is good for you*. Greater Good. https://greatergood.berkeley.edu/article/item/5_ways_giving_is_good_for_you

UCL. (2020, April 28). *10 benefits of helping others*. Students. https://www.ucl.ac.uk/students/news/2020/apr/10-benefits-helping-others

Wikipedia. (2022, June 8). *Count your blessings (instead of sheep)*. Wikipedia. https://en.wikipedia.org/wiki/Count_Your_Blessings_(Instead_of_Sheep)

Win at Life. (2015, July 23). *Bounce back from problems with the five minute rule*. Medium. https://medium.com/@WinatLifeGuide/bounce-back-from-problems-with-the-five-minute-rule-989cfc29c2e4

World Health Organization. (2021, September 13). *Depression*. WHO. https://www.who.int/news-room/fact-sheets/detail/depression#:~:text=At%20its%20worst%2C%20depression%20can

Printed in Great Britain
by Amazon